Partial Recall

Partial Recall

edited by

LUCY R. LIPPARD

with essays on

PHOTOGRAPHS OF NATIVE NORTH AMERICANS

by

Suzanne Benally   Ramona Sakiestewa

Jimmie Durham   David Seals

Rayna Green   Paul Chaat Smith

Joy Harjo   Jaune Quick-To-See Smith

Gerald McMaster   Gail Tremblay

Jolene Rickard   and Gerald Vizenor

Preface by

Leslie Marmon Silko

The New Press
New York, 1992

The New Press
New York, 1992

Copyright © 1992 by Lucy R. Lippard

Published in the United States by The New Press, New York
Distributed by W.W. Norton & Company, Inc.
500 Fifth Avenue, New York, NY 10110

Library of Congress Cataloging-in-Publication Data
Partial recall / edited by Lucy R. Lippard ; with essays on photographs of Native
    Americans by Suzanne Benally . . . [et al.].—1st ed.
        p.   cm.
Includes bibliographical references.
ISBN 1-56584-016-X : $29.95.—ISBN 1-56584-041-0 (pbk.) : $19.95
1. Indians of North America—Portraits.   2. Indians of North America—Pictorial
works.   3. Indians of North America—Ethnic identity.   I. Lippard, Lucy
R.   II. Benally, Suzanne.
E89.P33   1992
970.004'97—dc20   92-33710
CIP
First Edition
Book design by Bethany Johns Design

Printed in Mexico

Established in 1990 as a major alternative to the large, commercial publishing houses, The New Press is intended to be the first full-scale nonprofit American book publisher outside of the university presses. The Press is operated editorially in the public interest, rather than for private gain; it is committed to publishing in innovative ways works of educational, cultural, and community value, which despite their intellectual merits might not normally be "commercially viable."

Cover: **William Wildschut,** *White Swan*, Crow, Montana.
(Courtesy of the National Museum of the American Indian, Smithsonian Institution.)

Dedicated to the Native people pictured here.

ACKNOWLEDGMENTS

Thanks first and foremost to Jaune Quick-To-See Smith, Kay Miller, Jimmie Durham, Jolene Rickard, Ramona Sakiestewa, Peter Jemison, Suzanne Benally, and Gerald McMaster. They have taught me a lot about how much more I have to learn.

The support of Sharon Dean, Laura Nash, and the staff of the Photo Archive at the National Museum of the American Indian in New York was invaluable. Moira Roth, Anne Hockmeyer, Michelle Stuart, and especially Caroline Hinkley helped me make the last hard choices from hundreds of photographs, when I wanted to use them all. Alex Sweetman's book collection opened new pages. Rod Slemmons assisted in finding elusive photographs. David Sternbach has been an expert and good-humored editor, supporting the project from the beginning. Bethany Johns has contributed an elegant design.

And Anne Twitty brought this book out of the shadows.

Photo sources are in parentheses; when name of subject, photographer, date, or place is unknown, it is omitted. NMAI/SI: Courtesy of the National Museum of the American Indian/Smithsonian Institution, New York; DPL/WHC: Courtesy of the Denver Public Library/Western History Collection; CHS: Courtesy of the Colorado Historical Society, Denver.

All royalties from *Partial Recall* will be given to the American Indian College Fund.

CONTENTS

Leslie Marmon Silko

I have been around trays of developer and hypo under red safe lights since I was old enough to perch on a high stool. My father, Lee H. Marmon, learned photography in the Army. But to me it is still magic. The more I read about the behavior of sub-atomic particles of light, the more confident I am that photographs are capable of registering subtle electromagnetic changes in both the subject and the photographer. Professor Konomi Ara, my Japanese translator, photographed me outside my house in Tucson. Months later, when I saw the photograph in a Japanese publication, I was amazed and delighted to see how "Japanese" I appeared. How does this happen? Perhaps the way the photographer feels about her subject affects the outcome. Professor Ara had spent three years translating my novel *Ceremony* into Japanese; thus, in a few seconds, she was able to translate my face into Japanese.

Perhaps photographs register ambient bursts of energy in the form of heat or x-rays as well as light. Thus photographs reveal more than a mere image of a subject, although it is still too early for us to understand or interpret all the information a photograph may contain. In the summer and fall of 1980, I felt strangely inclined to take roll after roll of black and white film with a cheap autofocus camera. Obsessively, I photographed the dry wash below my ranchhouse. Stone formations with Hohokam cisterns carved in them appeared as sacred cenotes, and flat-top boulders looked as if they were sacrificial altars. Then, after the summer storms, I began to photograph certain natural configurations of stones and driftwood left by the floodwater. The photographic images of the stones and wood reminded me of glyphs. I could imagine there were messages in these delicate arrangements left in the wake of the flash flood. As I began to look at the prints, I realized each roll of film formed a complete "photo-narrative," although that had not been my intention as I pressed the shutter-release. Most of these narratives were constructed from the images of the "glyphs" I "saw" in the debris in the bottom of the arroyo.

One roll of film is memorable and horrifying in the clarity of its photographic images: this roll narrates what I can only see now as the abduction and murder of a woman or child whose body is buried in a shallow grave in the desert. There is a menacing black sedan parked incongruously in the bottom of the dry wash near a trail; at the time I snapped the picture, the car did not seem ominous. And at the time I photographed the big spider web gleaming in the weeds at the base of an ocotillo, I had no idea how much like a sunken, shallow grave the spider web would appear on film.

The origin of waves or particles of light-energy which may give such a sinister cast to a photograph is as yet unexplained. Fields of electromagnetic force affect light. Crowds of human beings massed together emanate actual electricity. Individual perceptions and behavior are altered. Witnesses report feeling an "electricity" that binds and propels a mob as a single creature. So the greed and violence of the last century in the U.S. are palpable; what we have done to one another and to the Earth is registered in the very atmosphere and effect, even in the light. "Murder, murder," sighs the wind over the rocks in a remote Arizona canyon where they betrayed Geronimo.

Geronimo was photographed immediately after his arrest in Skeleton Canyon. In this book, Cherokee artist Jimmie Durham writes, "Geronimo had the right to be hopeless and crazy, to be reduced to a passive beggar like so many Indian people at the time. Yet even when he was finally captured, he reportedly said, 'So you have captured me; the Mexicans would have killed me.' Then he looks at the camera, at the 'audience,' and tells us he will continue to resist." Durham chose to write about a photograph of Geronimo made after he had been imprisoned for years at Fort Sill, Oklahoma. In a fine top hat and vest, he sits behind the wheel of a new Cadillac. Durham writes, "Later, in the 20th century, when he is not allowed a rifle or his chaparral, he puts on your hat, takes the wheel, and stares the camera down. This photo makes clear that no matter what had been taken from him, he had given up nothing."

When Gerald McMaster looks at a photograph of students at a Canadian Industrial School for Indians, he sees that "these boys appear defiant. I was intrigued by their apparent ambivalence about being photographed, indicated by clenched fists or folded arms. Despite their cropped hair and foreign clothes, an element of individuality persists . . . These boys represented the colonial experiment, a type of colonial alchemy, transforming the savage into a civilized human. Yet somehow their resistance remains visible."

A fearless scholar who treads where few others dare, Lucy Lippard delights in stripping away comfortable images and clichés about photography and about Native Americans. In *Partial Recall*, she expands the aesthetic and perceptual boundaries of Western European art history as she invites twelve Native American artists and writers to write about the influences photographic images have had in the formation of Native American identity. Not since Susan Sontag's *On Photography* have there been such original and daring statements about photography. For instance— David Seals' discussions of sexism and racism in some Indian men. He admires the Scottish photographer, Sarah Penman, who rides in sub-zero temperatures to photograph Wounded Knee riders commemorating the massacre. Seals' point is that the spiritual integrity of the person behind the camera matters most. The people of my great-grandmother's generation were concerned less with a person's ancestry than with a person's integrity. Generosity and honesty were always more important than skin color in the old days before so many terrible crimes were committed.

Victor Masayesva (quoted in the introduction) points out how the camera "worships" and honors the ancient spirit beings and sacred ceremonies by averting its Eye, so that Hopi photographers display their reverence not only with the images they make, but also with the images they choose not to make. At Hopi, thoughtful action of any sort becomes worship; devoted attentiveness becomes worship. Ramona Sakiestewa writes with such beauty and passion about weaving that I imagined I had a flash of insight into the sensuous relationship the weaver enjoys with all the delicious textures. There is a difference between Jo Mora's intricate depictions and photographs by voyeurs/vampires like Curtis, Voth, and Vroman. That difference is love. Only one who loves Hopi weaving the way Sakiestewa does can see that Mora, too, loves weaving, that his photographs are a celebration of the beauty and complexity of the woven sashes and kilts, not some ethnographic document of the dancers' figures or actions.

Another of my favorite essays in *Partial Recall* is Rayna Green's brilliant explication of a Victorian-era photograph taken by a Japanese photographer of two Indian girls posed in the fashion of the day on a fainting couch. She gives us a witty recapitulation of the brief history of American Indians and the photographic image, concluding: ". . . these ladies have got no small measure of bravado. And not the 'it's-a-good-day-to-die' kind. I appreciate that often necessary and brave machismo, given circumstances, but there might have been other ways of weathering the storm. These girls have got it. Matsura saw it. What's more, he took its picture."

Indians are changed, but in control, and not always poor either. Joy Harjo's delightful story about the photograph of Marsie Harjo at the wheel of the big Hudson he always drove reveals the diversity of Native American experience. Oil money made it possible for one generation of Harjos to live in luxury. Without this photograph we might forget that Marsie Harjo's wife Katie was descended from the great Muscogee leader Monahwee, and that the fertile farmlands of Alabama had made all the Muscogee people rich until the white man came.

Five hundred years after the Native American holocaust began with Columbus' arrival, too many of us Indians are still here. We all know the story: Sixty to eighty million people died in the first one hundred years. But now Mexico City is the most populous city on earth, and the millions and millions who live there are Indians and mestizos. It is only a matter of time before the indigenous people of the Americas retake their land from the invaders, just as the African tribal people have repossessed nearly all the continent. Five hundred years is not much when compared to the fifteen thousand years Native Americans have lived on these continents. Thousands of years were necessary for the people to learn how to live *with* the land to survive and even thrive during the most difficult droughts and climate changes.

Great climatic changes are also underway today; on this point all can agree. Is it the "greenhouse effect" from fossil fuels, a consequence of above-ground nuclear tests, or is it simply another dimension of some ancient cycle of the Earth? Los Angeles, Las Vegas, San Diego, Phoenix, and Tucson are cities in the desert; supplies of potable water for these cities are dwindling fast. Maybe the newcomers need another five hundred or even a thousand years to learn how to live with the Earth here, but when the water has run out, their time will have run out too. Who will be left? Only a few remember how the desert nourishes her children who live with her. When they look at photographs of Los Angeles or Las Vegas, they will be amazed that the strangers lasted as long as they did.

From 1950 to the present my father has photographed the land and the people of the Laguna-Acoma area. Sometimes the families of the old folks would ask him to come. He used available light because he knew the old folks would be more comfortable without flashes, so usually the photographs were made outside. The old-time people liked to spend most of their time outdoors anyway. My father liked to take informal portraits: the old man with his prize watermelon, the old woman with her ovenbread on a board. He knew that these old folks, who had loved him and watched out for him as a child, would pass on to Cliff House soon. We all meet there at Cliff House someday, but I think my father couldn't bear to wait that long to see their beloved faces again.

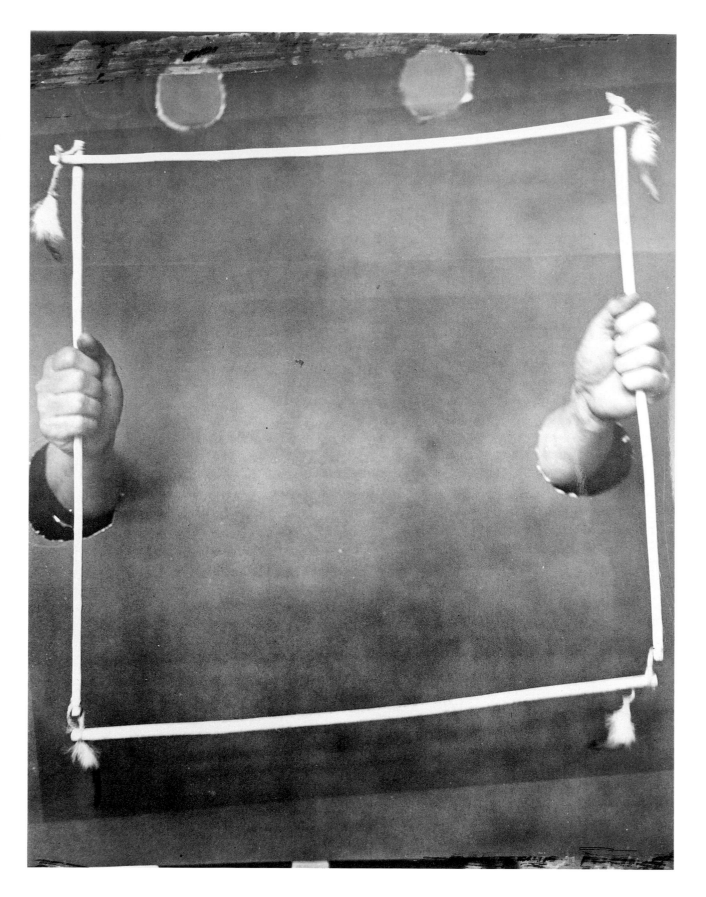

Washington Mathews (?), *Talisman of the Yebitsai, Open,* Navajo, c. 1902.

(NMAI/SI 7341.)

Lucy R. Lippard

I N T R O D U C T I O N

> *Photography is a philosophical sketching that makes it possible to define and then to understand our ignorance. Photography reveals to me how it is that life and death can be so indissolubly one; it reveals the falseness of maintaining these opposites as separate. Photography is an affirmation of opposites. The negative contains the positive.*
>
> —Victor Masayesva[1]

Part I: Partial Recall

This book was directly inspired by a single image. In the summer of 1990, Gerald McMaster sent me a postcard from Banff—a photo of an Assiniboine couple sitting in the grass with their little girl—and it began to haunt me. Within a month I found myself writing a long essay about this picture (see Part II, p. 34). The experience was so revelatory that I thought I would write a series of pieces, each departing from an individual photograph of Native North Americans. Eventually, however, after some political and professional work with Native friends, as well as a series of dreams, I realized that I should practice what I've been preaching. In my last book, *Mixed Blessings: New Art in a Multicultural America*, I insisted that white people need to surrender the "right" to represent everybody, the "colonial overview." So this book became a collaboration with those for whom these images had more intimate meanings. My own projected ten essays dwindled to this one, as a number of significant Native American writers and artists agreed to participate. They chose the photographs they would write about. The variety of images and texts that came in proves the power of merging distant and recent memories in response to a single frame.

The title is *Partial Recall* because total recall is impossible, even under the best of conditions. The past is hidden from us for many reasons, among them social amnesia and the absence of public images containing any more than fragments of real experience. The pasts of Native peoples in what is now North America are doubly obscured by the imposition of the myths of conquest, of the American West, and by the invention of new authenticities, the "discoveries" that have been much in mind during 1992, the five hundredth anniversary of Cristóbal Colón's accidental invasion of the Americas. As we look *inside* the images that have survived since photography appeared in the mid-nineteenth century—especially those taken since 1888, when the introduction of the Kodak box camera opened the field to everyone—we can at least sense vicariously the intersections of, and the differences between, the mythic Wests of white culture and of Native cultures.

In the space between the moments in which the photographs in this book were taken and the moment in which we look at them now, the differing communal desires have undoubtedly changed character, but they have not disappeared. We have been constantly reinventing these pictures ever since a photographer "took" the first Native's image in the mid-1840s. On the positive side of this continuing obsession is the possibility that with fresh interpretations, especially from Native people, new windows into these images will be opened; the lives and beliefs of the people depicted will be released from the prisons of the colonial past into a shared present. But, once apprehended, the pictures do not simply surrender their secrets. Instead, the calm flow of paternalistic history is eddied and diverted. New paradoxes emerge from the forest of grays.

If anyone has a right to nostalgia, to romanticize the past, it is Indians. But for obvious reasons, their view of historical photography (most of which was made "after the fall," in any case), tends to be skeptical, and even casual. Too many of these pictures, whatever truths they may hold, have been mendaciously manipulated. It is, therefore, white people who tend to look with greater longing at the past not quite depicted here. It represents for some of us a national childhood, when we were always right because we outpowered everyone and the burden of our murderous mistakes had yet to weigh on our collective conscience. For others it represents the death of an idealized "golden age." Buried in the pride of past conquest, less accessible than guilt and shame, is a distorted memory of primeval contentment. This too reflects a childhood, if not our own—playing cowgirls and Indians—then that of humanity. Many contemporary Euro-Americans (myself included) see in the hundreds of Native cultures of this continent spiritual and ethical values that have gone unnoticed or been neglected in our own culture. But there is another, deeper, desire involved. And that, I suspect, is the desire to *be* "the other," a kind of cultural cannibalism that is still being played out in our popular culture.

The hybridization and syncretization of global cultures that we are rediscovering today began in earnest in 1492.

As Indian people struggle at all social levels to be recognized as active subjects rather than passive objects in the ongoing history of this country, photographs play a significant role. Cracking their surfaces, breaking them open to get at the living content that has been erased from our history books is a challenging task. The "gallery" of additional photographs in this book (pp. 127–94) is the intensely personal result of long hours spent in libraries and historical archives in Denver, New York, Santa Fe, and Brunswick, Maine. Few famous or even familiar photographs are included. There are no mid-nineteenth-century images because the candid or vernacular views I was looking for were made more common by later technology.

My research was almost entirely pictorial, and many of these pictures are undated, unplaced, almost unanchored. I was looking for incongruous, atypical images of cross-cultural interaction and Native life in transition, images in which familiar expectations are jolted slightly off-center. Despite postmodernist warnings about "aestheticization," I am (as someone who earns her living writing about art) attracted to striking images and compositions, the odd gesture, the extraordinary face, the art of clothing . . . Yet I tried to focus on those images that have a more mysterious attraction, that are not necessarily picturesque or pictorially arresting, but bring with them across the years and cultural abysses something indefinably disturbing to the smugness of our current views of "Indians." The captions are brief in order to give the viewer the same provocative experience of "reading into a picture" enjoyed by the writers of this anthology.

It is a curious experience to go through the photographic archives—files and dusty files of pictures of people, most of them now dead. So few of the subjects are identified—not by Indian name, colonial name, or even by tribal affiliation. They are like ghosts deprived of rest. The photographers (they too are often anonymous) have put the subjects on the historical map, often falsifying forever a person's place in the world. There are many reasons for this—from the subjects' justified fears and resentments, to some photographers' ignorance and indifference to scholarship. Many of these images were also propaganda—taken not only to record "vanishing" indigenous cultures, but also to grease the wheels of assimilation.[2]

The photos are formal and candid, labeled and unlabeled, crisp or faded and torn. Wispy, fragile fragments of lives. In part because of social discomfort, and in part because of long exposure times, most of the portraits lack gesture; the bodies are wooden, turned lifeless. Even when the person is merely intended as a manne-

L. C. McClure, *Descending Trail from Indian Village of Acoma, N.M.* (with photographer carrying equipment). (DPL/WHC F26503.)

quin, a simulacrum, laden with jewelry and costume, even when the photographer is focusing on activity rather than person, even when the faces are resistant and "expressionless," the eyes cannot be veiled and humanity asserts itself. Far from the legendary impassivity, the subjects' expressiveness is often startling. The brutal scientific "objectivity" of the photographic process could not always overcome their visual insistence. Some faces, although unnamed, turn up in other books, other files, perhaps years older or younger. Some who are named appear to have changed so drastically in other images that the naming must be inaccurate. Others flash by and never reappear.

Nevertheless, the dehumanizing aspect of portrait photography as mere inventory is undermined by the irreducible presence of a self. A face, a gesture, a place, will suddenly stop me in my tracks. And although I look back over my shoulder to follow the path that led me to this place, it usually disappears into the trees, around the curve in the canyon, over the cusp of a hill, and I am lost in the present again, confronting the ratio of social construction inherent in any process of looking.

Sometimes I have questioned my own motives in choosing these pictures—*La Pinta*, for example (p. 128). As a woman, am I responding to the abstract beauty, or identifying with the human tragedy of a young woman whose skin is pigmentally disfigured, who has been asked to undress and stand, back to the camera, head bowed in shame, her clothes in a heap beside her, facing a weathered stone wall which echoes the patterns of her own graceful body? Probably both. And why does the young, and then the old, face of Zerviah Mitchell (pp. 162–63), a Wampanoag descendent of Massasoit who appears to carry African blood, hypnotize me across a century, when I had not wanted to include any classical portraits? This, and a few other portraits proved irresistible. From the hundreds of pictures I xeroxed and considered for this selection, certain faces, like those of Mitchell, and those of Sampson, Leah, and Frances Louise Beaver in the Banff postcard, pulled at me with such intensity that they would remain only briefly on the discard pile before they were restored.

A photograph is a passageway. Some photographs are dead ends. Others open into astonishing vistas and memories that cannot be owned. I find it useful when looking at photographs to try to enter that liberated space, to circumvent the barriers set up by unfamiliar culture and false history, to reach for a physical, tangible, sensuous experience of the image. This is not to say, of course, that I can "put myself in the subject's place." (I often have trouble doing that even when the subject of a photograph is myself—a figure I sometimes have trouble recognizing.) I am only grasping for the things we might have had in common, like the feeling of soft dry dust between the toes and the baking earth or brittle dry grass under the soles of the feet. Like the scratchy warmth of a handwoven blanket, the weight of an iron kettle, the heat of a cooking fire, the touch of a buckskin dress against bare skin. The bone-stiffening damp of a long trek through the snow, a horse's muscles gathering to run. The smells of pine trees and fresh wind, cool mist on the cheeks. Sore feet, sore back, from walking too long with a heavy burden.

This book is an attempt to recognize the reciprocity in the process of looking at history through images. Stereotypes boomerang. As the old children's ditty has it: "I'm rubber and you're glue; everything you say bounces off me and sticks to you." An 1871 newspaper article called Native people "vermilion strangers" in their own land and noted "the dignified bearing peculiar to the red men."[3] James Baldwin wrote almost thirty years ago, about being called a nigger: "If I am not what I've been told I am, then it means that *you're* not what you thought *you* were *either*! And that is the crisis."[4]

C. G. Morledge, *Pine Ridge Agency, S.D.* (staged conflicts).
(DPL/WHC F8941; 8852.)

Confronting that crisis means avoiding the well-trod paths of theoretical tourism, while facing up to the impossibility of totally evading them. It is not easy to divest ourselves—whoever we are—of treasured clichés concerning Native Americans. These pictures bring back a storm of colonial emotions, which have to be sorted out from more progressive responses. And demythologizing can bring disillusionment as well—a good thing, since illusions of any kind of "perfection" (nobility, impassivity, pantheistic connectedness, or authenticity) are obstacles to political freedom for the subjects. A feminist reading of myths about Indian people recognizes the pedestal-and-gutter syndrome, in which those whose righteous anger is threatening are placed beyond the pale—above it all or below it all. At the same time there is considerable dignity and resistance in many of these pictures which must not be mistaken for dime store "nobility" and torn away with the colonial packaging.

Looking at these photographs, even those taken within my lifetime, is a process of imagination, no matter how hardnosed the intended analysis. I look at them as though it were a mutual encounter. But in fact there are three of us involved. Between me as subject and subject as subject and both of us as objects of this inquiry are the photographers—our mediums, whether we like it or not. Few are Native Americans, although they too had cameras, and took family pictures that differ from outsiders' images primarily in their intimacy and casualness.[5] The photographers whose names we know are virtually all white men, although apparently many women also ran photo businesses in the nineteenth and early twentieth centuries.[6] Wives and daughters often carried on the trade while the men were away or after they died. Other women took up photography on their own, but had less access to adventure, money, and publicity. Much of their work probably ended up above the credit line of male photographers. (The same thing happened to men who worked for other men, so attribution is a confusing task.)

The biographies of "frontier photographers" strikingly parallel the stereotypes of today's macho, reckless, charming, and desperate journalists as apotheosized in the

H. S. Poley, *The Messenger: Severo on Horseback Telling Buckskin Charlie*, 1894.
(DPL/WHC P178; P185.) Another posed image, of Ute chiefs, retouched (or painted
over) to omit the suburban background and a group of people at left; a pot and fire
have been added to foreground. The altered version is signed "Chas. Craig, 1898."
Craig (1846–1931) was a painter specializing in western subjects.

movies (Nick Nolte in *Under Fire*, James Woods in *Salvador*, Linda Hunt and Mel
Gibson in *The Year of Living Dangerously*). They "shot" wars and Indian raids and
dragged their fragile, heavy equipment over mountain passes to document the
latest "discoveries." Months of work was lost when a horse slipped in a river or
a trail gave way beneath a pack mule. The women tended toward quieter themes,
although the enigmatic Kate Cory, who lived at Hopi from 1905 to 1912, took
the only pictures of the 1906 showdown between the Friendlies and the Hostiles
at Oraibi (p. 154).

The indigenous tragedy of a people surviving genocide, orphaned, displaced,
and largely deculturated in their own homeland, is *the* tragedy of this country, af-
fecting everyone far more than most of us realize. It lies buried, invisible beneath
the histories (plural, multidimensional) taught in schools and universities, beneath
the history (singular, one-dimensional) officially assumed, even beneath the stories
of lives lived and experienced individually, locally. It is the bump under the carpet
of colonialism, the nightmare at the edge of communal sleep.

While it is true that, as Cherokee Jimmie Durham tells us, Indians are not part
of our "rich cultural heritage,"[7] there is a common legacy even for those of us
whose ancestors emigrated to North America centuries after the initial damage
was done. Most of us do not even know it is our tragedy too. But when we read
the histories, and the ecological histories, many of us have to wonder, what is that
overwhelming sadness, as though it were our own lives lost, our own places devastated? As we peruse old photographs from a century's distance, we are all looking not only at but for something. That something varies among Euro-Americans
and Native people. It is often necessary to pry up the surfaces of apparent pathos,
as well as apparent pride, and to dig out from beneath something less accessible.

H. S. Poley, *Ute Indians at Play—Posing*, 1894. (DPL/WHC P33.) Towee, the wife of Chief Buckskin Charlie, is in front of the tipi. The other woman may be Kitty Cloud. She was married to Jim Taylor, the black cowboy on the ground, who was a well-known figure in his day.

Many of the contributors to this book talk more about what is *not* in these pictures than what *is*, because only through personal and historical contextualization can we fill in the blanks left by incomplete and mythologized histories.

If context is all-important, it is also usually out of reach. Place is an integral part of these images even when there is no landscape evident, even when there is "no there there," since many of the locations are unrecorded, lost to us. So understanding these photographs is a process of reaching out for what finally is absent, rather than grasping the presence of new "truths" and disseminating new "information." If the late twentieth-century Euro-American's perception of place is almost irreconcilably different from that of indigenous peoples, it is still necessary to acknowledge the histories of the places we live in, and the identity of our early "hosts."

Vine Deloria calls early twentieth-century photography

a weapon in the final skirmishes of cultural warfare in which the natives of North America could be properly and finally embedded in their places in the cultural evolutionary incline. . . . One must probe very deeply into the recesses of today's psyche to see the subtle tones of

*racism in the perpetual fascination of white Americans for portraits of Indians. That racism
. . . has a dualistic nature. . . . One encounters the substance of nobility and on returning to
the commonplace of daily life is a little irritated that things today cannot have the grandeur of
yesteryear, when simplicity and profundity shared the same bed.*[8]

Like Deloria, Hopi photographer and video artist Victor Masayesva also sees the
camera as a weapon in the process of photographic colonization, one "that will
violate the silences and secrets so essential to our group survival."[9] For him, the
camera and the missionary were tools, equally dangerous to group well-being.
Masayesva's view is supported by the firsthand testimony of a Hopi predecessor,
Don Talayesva, as told to anthropologist Leo Simmons in the late 1930s and
early 1940s:

> *The land was very dry, the crops suffered, and even the Snake dance failed to bring much
> rain. We tried to discover the reason for our plight and remembered the Rev. Voth who had
> stolen so many of our ceremonial secrets and even carried off sacred images and altars to equip
> a museum and become a rich man. . . . During the ceremonies this wicked man would force
> his way into the kiva and write down everything that he saw. He wore shoes with solid heels
> and when the Hopi tried to put him out of the kiva he would kick them. He came back to
> Oraibi on a visit. . . . Now I was grown, educated in the Whites' school, and had no fear of
> this man. . . . I said, "You break the commandments of your own God. He has ordered you
> never to steal or to have any other gods before him. He has told you to avoid all graven im-
> ages; but you have stolen ours and set them up in your museums. This makes you a thief and
> an idolator who can never go to heaven." . . . I had a strong desire to seize him by the collar
> and kick him off the mesa.*[10]

Masayesva also suggests an alternative role for the camera, inspired by cultural
conscience and tradition: "photography as ceremony, as ritual, something that
sustains, enriches, and adds to our spiritual well-being."[11] He learned from an
older Hopi man he was photographing to see himself as a Kwikwilyaqa kachina
clown—a figure that bears some physical resemblance to a camera and its ac-
coutrements. Yet a Kwikwilyaqa is also a nuisance, who duplicates, shadows those
in the plaza, and mimics their gestures and actions, conflating the activities of both
photographer and tourist. Masayesva acknowledges that Hopi photographers are as
eager as anyone else to capture the Snake dance and other ceremonials. But since
the camera's function doesn't change so drastically when it moves from white to
brown hands, for Native photographers, "refraining from photographing certain
subjects has become a kind of worship."[12]

Photography, loaded with historical stigmas, has only recently become an accepted art form among Indian peoples, although many have used the camera privately, as is demonstrated by several of the photographs the essayists have chosen,

T. Harmon Parkhurst, *Four Kossa Clowns, Mugging for the Photographer*, San Juan Pueblo, c. 1940. (Courtesy Museum of New Mexico, Santa Fe 3895.) "Left, Lorenzo Aquino?"

and by the testimony of Leslie Marmon Silko's book *Storyteller*.[13] There are not many Native photographers working as "artists" even today, although there are many more than is commonly recognized. This lack has been explained from within the communities as a response to past abuses. "Government surveyors, priests, tourists, and white photographers were all yearning for the 'noble savage' dressed in full regalia, looking stoic and posing like a Cybis statue. . . . We cannot identify with these images," wrote Jaune Quick-To-See Smith in her introduction to the first national Native American photography exhibition in 1984.[14] Those who expect from contemporary Indian photography something revealingly *different* are usually disappointed. Hopi photographer Jean Fredericks says that "privately, many Hopis approve of photography and want pictures of their families and celebrations, just like anyone else. Publicly, many feel they have to adopt a political position against photography. . . . This is to protect their privacy."[15] William

Jenkins, director of Northlight Gallery in Tempe, Arizona, which hosted the "Hopi Photographers" show, wrote:

The Hopi photographers clearly did not accept the pursuit of the "new" as a platform for the making of art. . . . The photographers seem concerned rather that the picture be "true": to themselves, to their subjects, to their beliefs, and to their culture.[16]

Many indigenous photographers bring to their art a simplicity that recalls the form's beginnings. The picture is valued for what it portrays. Losing its modernist identity as an image and its postmodernist identity as a reflection, it works in relation to another value system. This notion may make the "sophisticated" uneasy, since it disregards the common, postmodern perception that a photo cannot tell the truth. Perhaps it can never tell the whole truth and is often used to tell lies, but there is always at least a grain of truth in a moment that did take place, and it is against that grain that we must test our eyesight.

Alone with my campfire, I gaze about on the completely circling hilltop, crested with countless campfires, around which are gathered the people of a dying race. The gloom of approaching night wraps itself about me. I feel that the life of these children of nature is like the dying day drawing to its end; only off in the West is the glorious light of the setting sun, telling us, perhaps, of light after darkness.

—Edward Curtis, 1905[17]

Although I studiously avoided his images in the "photo gallery" of this book, photographs of Native Americans cannot be discussed without confronting the monumental figure of Edward Curtis, imperfect hero of the genre and victim of the demythologizing trends of the 1980s. If his work was hardly, as A. D. Coleman wrote in a burst of enthusiasm in 1972, "the most profound document of pure Indian culture ever made,"[18] the alternative image that has emerged in recent years of Curtis as no more than a romantic exploiter and faker of the Indian past is also unjust. Edward Curtis, with a grade-school education, spent thirty years of his life taking the forty thousand photographs of over eighty tribes that culminated in the twenty volumes of *The North American Indian*. While mistaken in his conviction that he was recording the last days of a "vanishing race," he was right in believing that his photographs would be invaluable (not infallible) documents of a historical process of representation.

Curtis was not a tourist. He was apparently trusted by many of the people he lived with and documented. He studied for months before each visit, sent an agent ahead to prepare the people for his arrival, and when he came, he sometimes stayed and often returned. He traveled and lived under the most rigorous circumstances and, aside from the glory days when he was sponsored by the likes of J. P. Morgan and Teddy Roosevelt, he made great financial sacrifices which led to divorce and

Edward Curtis, *San Ildefonso: Pinch of Corn Offered to Deities; Formality to Begin the Tewa Day* (Courtesy The Library of Congress, Washington D.C., LC-45Z62-61129).

an impecunious old age. Curtis is erroneously credited with presenting the private side of reluctantly public individuals. Yet when he was about halfway through his magnum opus, the Native nations began to see the importance his work might have for their own future generations. "The ordinary investigator going among them to secure information for a magazine article, they do not favor," Curtis observed. "But they have grasped the idea that this is a permanent memorial of their race, and it appeals to their imagination. . . . Tribes that I won't reach for four or five years yet have sent me word asking me to come and see them."[19] Still, he was shot *at* four times, once left a camp in the dead of night when a little girl he had photographed died from a fall, and wrote: "I have grown so used to having people yell at me to keep out, and then punctuate their remarks with mud, rocks, and clubs that I pay but little attention to them if I can only succeed in getting my picture before something hits me."[20]

As A. D. Coleman has observed, Curtis was an unabashed interpreter. But "just as Edward Curtis stole the spirit of the Indians, they in turn stole his."[21] Curtis was, finally, an artist, with all the implied freedoms and shortcomings that come with that title; he even presented one of the first mixed-media events in his 1911 *Indian Picture Opera*, a narrative incorporating film and music. He also wrote two best-sellers, made a unique film in which the Kwakiutl helped him recreate scenes from their past, and recorded on wax over ten thousand songs from around the country. In addition, he has inadvertently provided us with a target on which to focus our changing notions of "authenticity."

Curtis is attacked most often, and most legitimately, for his lack of ethnographic veracity. His soft focus blurred what might have been important details. He staged scenes, routinely retouched and faked night skies, storm clouds, and other dramatic lighting effects.[22] He erased unwelcome signs of modernity, although late in life he finally became resigned to change and photographed people as they were. In his heyday, however, he was an emotional formalist, not an objective documentarian. Curtis was distressed when he arrived "too late" and found customs and ceremonials no longer in use. With the help of the tribes, he sometimes recreated them. When working in the Pacific Northwest, he carried with him wigs (for those who now had white man's haircuts), "primitive" clothes, and other out-of-date trappings. Cedar-bark capes were made for him by Kwakiutl people. Navajo Yebichai, worried about being photographed, actually "insisted that Curtis make their costumes himself so the clothing would not have a religious significance."[23]

Vine Deloria was justifiably outraged when a senator he was lobbying on Indian rights claimed he "knew a great deal about Indians" and shoved a book of Curtis photographs across his desk. Deloria argues that since Curtis' photographs

did not in the slightest degree speak to the reality of the American Indian, either past or present, they became the perfect format for expression of the wistful reservoir of emotions that lay behind the general perceptions of Indians. If people could not take cocoa and cookies to Dull Knife's fleeing Cheyenne and piously separate themselves from advocates of Manifest Destiny, they could at least mount a Curtis print prominently in their homes and silently proclaim their solidarity with Indians.[24]

Deloria also concedes that the Indian community itself has not been immune to such romanticization:

Drawn increasingly together as an ethnic group and away from their traditions as distinct communities with sometimes malevolent feelings toward other tribes, Indians saw in the Curtis pictures an opportunity to universalize the nobility and wisdom suggested there and claim it as a natural, sometimes even a genetic, Indian trait.

But by and large, Indians who have more experience with the manipulations of white culture "detested the fawning over Curtis":

They had previously experienced such periods of intense euphoria inspired by the white majority only to find the climate radically shifting and producing substantial hardships when people forgot their pledge of undying guilt toward the nation's first citizens. Thus a weak smile and an uncomfortable shrug was about the only response that Curtis pictures evoked in older Indians.[25]

Around the turn of the century, Indians were the photogenic counterparts of today's "lookouts"—roadside scenic vistas, ready-made "views," "nature" viewed from a static culture.[26] When people were (and are) photographed in the majestic landscape of the West, it is difficult to avoid some of the components of "romanticism"—awe and a sense of timelessness—that seem impossibly embedded in the landforms themselves (the "new topographers" who photograph the neutral and defiled West notwithstanding). The people living as part of such lands were endowed, however mistakenly and hypocritically, with the same qualities. Malek Alloula calls this colonizing approach a "vivesector's gaze":

As the imaginary accomplishment of a phantasm, [photography] carries within itself a principle of deception. . . . Photography nourishes the voyeurism of the photographer but never satiates it because the voyeurism, as the structure of desire, has neither beginning nor end.[27] *[The photographer becomes] sole owner of a closed space from which he absconds since he is nothing but gaze. For indeed, how is the voyeur to be defined if not as a gaze without presence or a gaze against a backdrop of absence?*[28]

The role of photography in tourism (or as tourism) started early. What looks to us today like a serious "documentary" photograph may just be the equivalent of *National Geographic* voyeurism, or a color print of a New York City homeless person made for the folks back home. Even today, when Zunis wear rubber boots or

Navajo Tribal Enterprise—The Tourists. (Courtesy Standard Oil of New Jersey.)

sneakers at Shalako, or when an Apache puberty ritual includes six-packs of soda among the offerings, tourists and purists tend to be offended. Such "anachronisms" destroy the time-honored distance between Them and Us, the illusion that They live in different times than We do. "Anachronisms" may also be somewhat threatening to Our peace of mind, recalling how They got There, were put There, in a space that is separated from Us by the barbed wire of "absentee colonialism" (see p. 135).

But how did *we* get *there*—off center—to the places where we are face-to-face with those who do not apparently resemble us? Johannes Fabian has distinguished between historic religious travel "*to* the centers of religion or *to* the souls to be saved" and today's secular travel "*from* the centers of learning and power to places where man was to find nothing but himself."[29] The Sioux visionary Black Elk says that anywhere can be the center of the world. We the "conquerors" have not thought so. We travel to the margins to fulfill some part of us that is "marginal" to our own culture, but becoming increasingly, embarrassingly, central.

Once at the margins, we are not welcomed with open arms. At ceremonial dances or secular powwows, we gawk or smile shyly at the Indian people hurrying by, and they ignore us or are politely aloof when spoken to, so long as we behave

Donald A. Cadzow, *Mission Slave Girl Washing*, Great Slave Lake, Northwest Territory, Canada. (NMAI/SI 5669.) The bland title fails to mention that the woman is trying to fend off the photographer.

ourselves. They don't need us but we somehow, paradoxically, need them. We need to take images away from these encounters, to take Them with Us. According to Dean MacCannell, tourists are trying to "discover or reconstruct a cultural heritage or a social identity. . . . Sightseeing is a ritual performed to the differentiations of society."[30] The same might be said of photography itself. In the archives there are many photographs of Native people hiding their faces or otherwise trying to avoid the camera. Initially, a picture being "shot" must have resembled all too closely a rifle being "shot" as the instrument was raised to the eyes and a "trigger" was pulled. Soon it was recognized as the ultimate invasion of social, religious, and individual privacy. When William Henry Jackson tried to take a panoramic photograph of the Ute village of Los Piños, the Indians, who saw his camera as "my strange box of bad medicine," kept heckling him:

As I attempted to focus, one of them would snatch the cloth from my head; or toss a blanket over the camera; or kick out one of the supporting legs.[31]

Then they demanded the negatives. He tried to hold on to them, but finally gave up. D. H. Thomas describes an appalling scene at Santo Domingo's Happiness Dance in 1926:

The men were warned not to attempt to take any pictures, even though the bright moon would permit it. There were two busloads on the tour, and as they drew up to the pueblo, full half the men grabbed their cameras, jumped off the bus, and started snapping away at the dancing Indians. Without a sound, Indians poured out of every doorway, all carrying clubs. The two drivers lit out at a dead run to round up the scattering men, but before they could get them back on the buses, there was a general smashing of cameras that started by knocking them to the ground with clubs and then jumping up and down on them.[32]

By the turn of the century, Indians were already officially protesting the presence of photographers. In 1902 the Hopi restricted photographers to a specific area so they could not interfere with the ceremonies. In 1910 they banned photography of the ceremonies altogether, as a result of a trip to Washington where they saw "a congressional hearing room plastered with a selection of photographs of religious ceremonies . . . [which] they found to their dismay, were being used by Bureau officials and missionaries to discredit their religion."[33] In 1911 photography was banned in the pueblos. Photography at the Walpi Snake Dance—the ceremony that most titillated outsiders—was finally forbidden officially by the Commissioner of Indian Affairs in 1915 and personally implemented by Rio Grande Pueblos Superintendent Leo Crane, who was angered by the disrespect shown by white photographers at the ceremonies. Some tourist entrepreneurs had even gone so far as to suggest changes in the ceremonies in order to make them more photogenic.

George L. Beam, *Dancers at Taos Pueblo.* (DPL/WHC F6010.) Here, too, the title ignores the angry dancer at left running toward the photographer.

At the same time, the dances themselves were being attacked. Into the 1920s, photographs of the ceremonies were used against Natives by people like Commissioner of Indian Affairs Charles Burke, who made certain ceremonial dances "Indian Offenses" in 1921.[34] Public and legal opposition to his Circular No. 1655 was immediate, and by 1928 the Bureau had backed down. Today photography is banned by many pueblos and reservations, especially in the Southwest. Its prohibition has been a major component in the slow process of regaining Native sovereignty, or self-determination:[35]

> WARNING WARNING NO OUTSIDE WHITE VISITORS ALLOWED BECAUSE OF YOUR FAILURE TO OBEY THE LAWS OF OUR TRIBE AS WELL AS THE LAWS OF YOUR OWN. THIS VILLAGE IS HEREBY CLOSED. *(Sign placed outside Old Oraibi in 1974 by Mina Lanza, "village chief" from 1960 until her death in 1978.)*[36]

Photographers were called "shadow catchers" by some tribes (the shadow referring to death, or the soul of the dead). The transfer of a black-and-white likeness

A. Richard King (?), "Avoidance behavior during picture taking. The girl holding the string game is the sixteen-year-old for whom there is no record of her early years at the Mopass school." (Photo and caption from A. Richard King, *The School at Mopass: A Problem of Identity* [New York: Holt, Rinehart, and Winston, 1967.] Mopass was a Protestant boarding school for Yukon Indians founded in 1901 in the Yukon Territory, Canada.)

to paper meant to some that a part of their lives had been taken away, to others that their vital power had been diminished. These beliefs have never fully disappeared. In 1984, Lillie Benally, the Navajo woman who posed in 1932 for Laura Gilpin's famous *Navajo Madonna*, sued the Amon Carter Museum in Fort Worth for its use of the image in museum publicity. She said she had agreed to have the photograph taken, but not to its publication, which could, according to traditional beliefs, have a harmful effect.[37]

When the young Alfred M. Bailey (later director of the Denver Museum of Natural History) was doing field work as a naturalist in Alaska in 1919, he asked a fisherman at the Tlingit village of Kake to pose for a picture. "He curtly refused and when I asked why, he said, 'You want to put it on a postcard and laugh at me.' "[38]

Photographs of Indians, adorned by patronizing and sometimes racist and sexist captions, were routinely made into postcards by the turn of the century, and still are, having become the populist counterpart of the coffee-table photo book as an aid to armchair tourism. Frank Matsura, the Japanese photographer who worked in Washington State in the early 1900s, had almost all of his photographs made into postcards and displayed hundreds of them in his studio, where they were sold along with "Oriental curios and gifts." Although Matsura's intimate, respectful, and extraordinarily sculptural images of Indians were an exception, the photographs of Native people finding their way onto commercial postcards today tend to be either reruns of Curtis and his contemporaries or "costume shots" bearing no resemblance to the daily life of Native people. In fact, many of them seem also to be reruns of pictures taken in the '50s and '60s before many pueblos and reservations banned photography. "Falsely naïve, the postcard misleads in direct measure to the fact that it presents itself as having neither depth nor aesthetic pretensions. *It is the 'degree zero' of photography*," writes Malek Alloula.[39]

Much that Alloula has written about orientalism and "the Colonial Harem" in his book of that name, is all too easily transposed to the photography of American Indians. He points out how the "ethnographic alibi"[40] leads to manipulative violence and fabricates a "pacified reality, restored to the colonial order."[41] When nineteenth-century orientalist painting ran out of wind, he says,

photography steps in to take up the slack and reactivates the phantasm at its lowest level. . . . The postcard does it one better; it becomes the poor man's phantasm: for a few pennies, display racks full of dreams. The postcard is everywhere, covering all the colonial space. . . . It produces stereotypes in the manner of great seabirds producing guano. It is the fertilizer of the colonial vision.[42]

Frontier photographers gleefully photographed Native women in various stages of undress, especially bare-breasted. If this was not their natural custom, they were often disrobed in the aid of prurient commercialism. Even women photographers went in for this "scientific" practice (see p. 169). Christopher Lyman suggests that the half-naked images "did not strike the white public as pornography only because their Indian subjects were generally thought to be less than human."[43] Similarly, Native people in traditional dress or large feathered warbonnets (often not worn by their own tribes) were constantly photographed in incongruous situations, such as playing golf, taking photographs, driving cars, flying planes.[44]

In a number of the pictures I found, the Native people are falsely "foregrounded," pushed up to the front row, to the photographic firing line. The backgrounds, however, pierce the surface, inhabited as they often are by whites— onlookers, bypassers, voyeurs (see pp. 137, 139). Thus white people are seen

Alanson B. Skinner, *A. B. Skinner and Cree Informant*, Rupert House, Ontario, Canada, 1916. (NMAI/SI 3659.)

through a screen of Indian images, the powers behind their backs. We, the camera, are offered an overview of watchfulness, the wariness, the witnesses, even as we too are accomplices in the manipulations. Pictures of the anthropologists with their informants are also illuminating. For instance, in *A. B. Skinner and Cree Informant at Rupert House, Ontario, 1916,* the aptly named Skinner is intent on committing to writing something the unnamed informant is showing him. Skinner himself is "in costume," wearing a jaunty checkered cap indoors. A bone and part of a skull lie before them on the table—a silent third participant in the process, the medium of information from the past, translated by the living descendant. Secrets or trivia or calculated half-truths are being passed into the voracious maw of the anthropologist's notebook. The Cree man, the visitor, is clearly the teacher, Skinner the avid student. Yet Skinner will be *our* informer, bringing over the border those snatches of another life that will tantalize and fascinate an audience of mostly white students and scholars for years to come. This is the part of the recall that is available to us to analyze and criticize. With the writers of this book as the agents, shreds of other parts are now becoming perceptible through the gloom and the celluloid curtain.

Mary Sharples Schaffer Warren, *Sampson, Frances Louise, and Leah Beaver,* 1907.
(Courtesy the Whyte Museum, Banff, British Columbia, Canada.)

Part II: Doubletake:
The Diary of a Relationship with an Image⁴⁵

First Take

Sam[p]son Beaver and his Family. This lovely photograph of Stoney Indian Sam[p]son Beaver was taken by Mary Schaffer in 1906. She was a writer, naturalist, photographer and explorer who lived and worked in the Rockies for many years. Mary Schaffer is one of several notable women who visited the area early in the century and fell captive to the charm of the mountains.

—Caption on contemporary postcard from Banff, Canada.

I am surprised by this photograph, which seems so unlike the conventional images I've seen of Native people "taken" by white people. It is simple enough—a man and woman are smiling warmly at the photographer while their little girl smirks proudly. The parents are seated comfortably on the ground, the man with his legs crossed, the woman perhaps kneeling. The child stands between them, closer to her father, holding a "bouquet" of leaves. Behind them are signs of early spring—a tree in leaf, others still bare-branched.

I'm examining my deep attraction to this quiet little picture. I have been mesmerized by these faces since the postcard was sent to me last month by a friend, a Native Canadian painter and curator who found it in a taxidermy/Indian shop (he was bemused by that conjunction). Or maybe I am mesmerized by the three cultural spaces between the Beaver family and Mary Schaffer and me.

They are not vast spaces, although we are separated at the moment by a continent, national borders, and eighty-four years. They consist of the then-present space of the subjects, the then-present, but perhaps very different, space of the photographer, and the now-present space of the writer in retrospect, as a surrogate for contemporary viewers. Or perhaps there are only two spaces: the relationship between photographer and subjects then, and between me/us and the photograph now. I wonder where these spaces converge. Maybe only on this page.

Good photography can *embody* what has been seen. As I scrutinize it, this photograph becomes the people photographed—not "flat death," as Roland Barthes would have it, but flat life. This one-way (and, admittedly, romantic) relationship is mediated by the presence/absence of Mary Schaffer, who haunts the threshold of the encounter. I am borrowing her space, that diminished space between her and the Beaver family. She has made a frontal (though not a confrontational) image, bringing her subjects visually to the foreground, into the area of potential intimacy. The effect is heightened by the photograph's remarkable contemporaneity, the crisp "presentness" which delivers this image from the blatant anthropological distancing evident in most photographs of the period. The Beavers' relaxed poses and friendly, unselfconscious expressions might be those of a contemporary snapshot, except for the high quality of the print. At the same time, they have been freed from the "ethnographic present"—that patronizing frame that freezes personal and social specifics into generalization, and is usually described from a neutral and anonymous third-person perspective. They are "present" in part because of their undeniable personal presence. A certain synchronism is suggested, the "extended present" or "eternal present" cited by N. Scott Momaday, among others.

What would happen to the West, Johannes Fabian has mused, "if its temporal fortress were suddenly invaded by the Time of its Other"?[46] I think I've been invaded. I feel as though I know these people. Sampson Beaver and his wife seem more familiar than the stiff-backed, blank-faced pictures of my own great-grandparents, the two pairs who went west in the 1870s and 1880s, among those pushing their way into others' centers from the eastern margins of the continent.[47] Five years ago, while I was despairing of ever finding the structure for a book about the cross-cultural process, I dreamed I was climbing a vast grassy hill toward a weather-beaten wooden cabin at the top; on its steps sat three Native people, silently encouraging me to keep going. Although they were elderly, the expressions on their faces were those of the young Beaver family in this photograph.

As I begin, I'm also looking at this triple portrait cut loose from all knowledge of the people involved—an aspect that normally would have informed much of my own position. With only the postcard's caption to go on, my response is not neutral, but wholly subjective. I'm aware that writing about a white woman photographing Native people is a kind of metaphor for my own position as an Anglo critic trying to write about contemporary Native North American art. I'd rather be Mary Schaffer, a courageous woman in long skirts who seems to be trusted by this attractive couple and their sweetly sassy child. How did she find her way past the barriers of turn-of-the-century colonialism to receive these serene smiles? And I want to be Sampson Beaver and his (unnamed) wife, who are so at home where they are, who appear content, at least in this spring moment.

Second Take

I showed the picture and my "diary" to a friend, who said she was convinced that the real relationship portrayed was between the photographer and the child, that the parents liked Schaffer because she had made friends with their little girl. Certainly the photograph implies a dialogue, an exchange, an *I/eye* (the photographer) and a *you* (her subjects)—and *we* the viewers, if the photographer would emerge from beneath her black cloth and turn to look back at us. At the same time, the invisible (unknowable) autobiographical component, the "viewpoint" provided by the invisible photographer, "writer, naturalist, . . . and explorer, who lived and worked in the Rockies for many years," is another factor that shaped what is visible here. I have written to the Whyte Museum of the Canadian Rockies, in Banff, for information about her.

The cultural abyss that had to exist in 1906 between the Beaver family and Mary Schaffer was (though burdened by political circumstances and colonial conditioning) at least intellectually unselfconscious. It may have been further diminished by what I perceive (or project) as the friendly relationship between them. The time and cultural space that usually distances me—self-consciously but involuntarily—from historic representations of Another is also lessened here. Schaffer's photograph lacks the rhetorical exposure of "authenticity." But the Beavers are not universalized into oblivion as "just folks," either. Their portrait is devoid of cuteness, and yet it has great charm. Despite the inevitable veneer of exoticism (a function of the passage of historical time and the interval implied by the dress of almost ninety years ago), it is only secondarily quaint. This is not, however, the Edward Curtis view of the Noble Savage, staring moodily into the misty past or facing the camera forced upon him or her with the wariness and hostility that has been co-opted by naming it "dignity."

It is now common to observe that one of the hegemonic devices of colonialism (postcolonialism is hardly free of it either) has been to isolate the Other in another time, a time that also becomes another place—The Past—even when the chronological time is the present. Like racism, this is a habit hard to kick even when it is recognized. Schaffer's photograph is a microcosmic triumph for social equality as expressed through representation. The discontinuity and disjunctiveness that usually characterize cross-cultural experience are translated here into a certain harmony—or the illusion thereof. This is a sympathetic photograph, but it is not, nor could it be, empathetic. (Is it possible to honestly perceive such a scene as idyllic within the dystopian social context?) The three figures, despite their smiles and amicable, knowing expressions, remain the objects of our gazes. We are simply lucky that this open, intelligent gaze has passed into history as alternative evidence of the encounter between Native and European, of the maintenance of some human interaction in the aftermath of genocide.

The Beavers' portrait seems a classic visualization of what anthropologists call "intersubjective time." It commemorates a reciprocal moment (rather than a cannibalistic one), where the emphasis is on interaction and communication; a moment in which subject and object are caught in exchange within shared time, rather than shouting across history from their respective peaks. The culturated distance between photographer and photographed, between white and Native, has somehow been momentarily bridged to such an extent that the bridge extends over time to me, to us, almost a century later.

This is the kind of photograph I have often used as an example of the difference between images taken by someone from within a community and by an "outsider." I would have put it in the former category. Yet it was not taken by a Stoney, but by an adventurous white lady passing through the northern Rockies, possibly on the quest for self (or loss of self) in relation to Other and Nature that has been a major theme in North American culture.

The Beaver family (I wish I knew the woman's and child's names) is clearly among friends, but the picture might still have been very different if taken by a Native insider. Of course we have no way of knowing what that image might have been. A press release from the American Indian Community House Gallery in New York in 1984 set out some distinctions between non-Indian and Indian photographers; among them: "These photos are not the universal images of Indians. They are not heroic, noble, stoic, or romantic. What they do show is human

warmth and an intimacy with their subject. . . ."[48] This is the feeling I get
from the Beavers' portrait. Am I just kidding myself? Overidentifying with
Mary Schaffer?

Another explanation for Native avoidance of photography raises old taboos—the
"photos-steal-your-spirit syndrome," which is not, in fact, so far off. The more we
know about representation, the more obvious it becomes that photography *is* often
a spirit snatcher. I "own" a postcard which permits me to "have" the Beaver family in my house. The Oglala warrior Crazy Horse never allowed his photograph to
be taken, and it was said of those Native leaders who did that "they let their spirits
be captured in a box" and lost the impetus to resist. Contemporary AIM leader
Russell Means has described the introduction of writing into oral traditions as a
destructive "abstraction over the spoken relationship of a people." As Dennis
Grady observes, the camera was another weapon in the wars of domination:

*How fitting it must have seemed to the victims of that process—the natives of North Amer-
ica, whose idea of "vision" is as spiritual as it is physical—when the white man produced
from his baggage a box that had the power to transcribe the world onto a flat paper plane.
Here was a machine that could make of this landscape a surface; of this territory, a map; of
this man, this woman, this living child, a framed, hand-held, negotiable object to be looked
at, traded, possessed; the perfect tool for the work of the "wasi'chu," the greedy one who
takes the fat.*[49]

Our communal "memory" of Native people on this continent has been projected through the above-mentioned stoic (*numb* is more like it), wary, pained, resigned, belligerent, and occasionally pathetic faces "shot" by nineteenth- and early
twentieth-century photographers like Edward Curtis, Adam Clark Vroman, and
Roland W. Reed—all men. Looking through a group of portraits of Indians from
that period, I found one (*Indian with Feather Bonnet*, c. 1898) in which the expression was less grim, more eye-to-eye; the photographer was Gertrude Käsebier (see
p. 168). The photographs by Kate Cory (a "midwestern spinster" who came to Arizona at age forty-four), taken in the Hopi village where she lived for seven years,
also diverge from the general pattern (see pp. 154, 173) as do Nancy Wood's contemporary images of Taos Pueblo (see pp. 131, 151) and some of Laura Gilpin's
works. All of which suggests empathy as a factor in the relationship between race
and gender lurking in this subject.

Of course Mary Schaffer, despite her gender, was at least indirectly allied with
the oppressors. She may have been an "innocent" vehicle of her class, her culture,
and her times. She may have been a rebel and independent of some of its crueler
manifestations. Less likely, she may have known about the then-new "comparative
method" of anthropological investigation, which was to permit the "equal" treat-

ment of all human culture in all times and in all places (though, of course, it failed to overturn the edifice of Otherness on which it was built). She may have been an enthusiastic perpetrator of expansionism.

Perhaps this photograph was already tinged with propaganda even at the time it was taken. Perhaps Mary Schaffer herself had an ax to grind. She may have been concerned to show her audience (and who were *they*?) that the only good Indian was not a dead Indian. Perhaps this portrait is the kind of "advocacy image" we find in the production of leftist photographers working in El Salvador. The knowledgeable, sympathetic tourist is not always immune to cultural imperialism. I wonder if Mary Schaffer, like so many progressive photographers working in poorer neighborhoods and countries, gave her subjects a print of this photograph. Was it their first, their only image of themselves? Or the first that had not disappeared with the photographer? Is a curling copy of this picture given a place of honor in some family photo album or on the wall of some descendent's home?

I'm overpersonalizing the depicted encounter. To offset my emotional attraction to this image, let me imagine that Schaffer was a flag-waving imperialist and try to read this image, or my responses to this image, in a mirror, as though I had taken an immediate dislike to it. Can I avoid that warm gaze and see in these three figures an illustration of all the colonial perfidy that provides its historical backdrop? Do Sampson Beaver and his family look helpless and victimized? They are handsome, healthy people, perhaps chosen to demonstrate that Indians were being "treated well." The family is seated on the ground, perhaps placed there because the photographer was influenced by stereotypical representations of the "primitive's" closeness to the earth. The woman is placed at a small distance from her husband and child—like a servant? They are smiling; perhaps Schaffer has offered the child a treat, or the adults some favor. Still, it is hard to see these smiles as solely money-bought.

A virtual class system exists among the common representations of an Indian family from this period: the lost, miserable, huddled group outside a tipi, the businesslike document of a neutrally "ordinary" family, or the proud, noble holdouts in a grand landscape, highlighted by giant trees or dramatic mesas. For all the separations inherent in such images, there is no such thing as "objectivity" or neutrality in portrait photography. Personal interaction of *some* kind is necessary to create the context within the larger frame of historical events. Even the Schaffer photo is "posed." And the pose is an imposition, since Native people had no traditional way of sitting for a portrait or a photograph; self-representation in that sense was not part of the cultures. But at least the Beaver family is not sitting bolt upright in wooden chairs; Sampson Beaver is not standing patriarchally with his hand on his wife's shoulder while the child is properly subdued below. Man and wife are comfortable and equal as they smile at the black box confronting them, and the little girl's expression is familiar to anyone who has spent time with little girls.

Today I received some scraps of information about the Stoney Indians, who were Assiniboine, offshoots of the Sioux. (The name is an anglicization based on the Ojibwa word *assine*, which means stone.) They called themselves Nakodah and arrived in the foothills of the Rockies in the eighteenth century, in flight from smallpox epidemics. With the advent of settlers and the founding of Banff, the Stoneys were forced into a life of relatively peaceful interaction with the townspeople. In the late nineteenth century, Banff was already a flourishing tourist town, boasting a spa and the annual "Indian Days" powwow, begun in 1889. The Whyte Museum there has a massive archive of photographs of the Native people of the Rockies (including this one, and one of Ginger Rogers on vacation, sketching Chief Jacob Twoyoungman in a Plains headdress). Eventually forced to live off of tourism, the Stoneys were exploited but not embattled. And Mary Schaffer, for all her credentials, was a tourist herself.

Last Take

The books ordered from Banff have finally arrived. I dove into them and of course had to revise some of my notions.

The Beaver family photograph was taken in 1907, not 1906; not in early spring, but in late September, as Schaffer was completing a four-month expedition to the sources of the Saskatchewan River. Having just crossed two turbulent rivers, she and her companions reached the "Golden Kootenai Plains," (the Katoonda, or Windy Plains) and, weaving in and out of yellowing poplars, they

spied two tepees nestled deep among the trees. . . . I have seen not one but many of their camps and seldom or never have they failed to be artistic in their setting, and this one was no exception. Knowing they must be Silas Abraham's and Sampson Beaver's families, acquaintances of a year's standing, I could not resist a hurried call. The children spied us first, and tumbling head over heels, ran to cover like rabbits. . . . Above the din and excitement I called, "Frances Louise!" She had been my little favorite when last we were among the Indians, accepting my advances with a sweet baby womanliness quite unlike the other children, for which I had rewarded her by presenting her with a doll I had constructed. . . . Love blinded the little mother's eyes to any imperfections, and the gift gave me a spot of my own in the memory of the forest baby. . . . In an instant her little face appeared at the tepee-flap, just as solemn, just as sweet, and just as dirty as ever.[50]

It was this group of Stoneys (members of the Wesley Band) who the previous year had given Schaffer her Indian name: Yahe-Weha, Mountain Woman. Banned from hunting in the National Parks, they were still able to hunt, trap, and live beyond their boundaries. In 1907 she remained with them for four days. Of this visit she wrote:

When I hear those "who know" speak of the sullen, stupid Indian, I wish they could have been on hand the afternoon the white squaws visited the red ones with their cameras. There were no men to disturb the peace, the women quickly caught our ideas, entered the spirit of the game, and with musical laughter and little giggles, allowed themselves to be hauled about and pushed and posed in a fashion to turn an artist green with envy. . . . Yahe-Weha might photograph to her heart's content. She had promised pictures the year before, she had kept the promise, and she might have as many photographs now as she wanted. [51]

Sampson Beaver's wife Leah was no doubt among the women that afternoon. He was thirty years old at the time, and she looks about the same age. In the latently desirous language of the tourist, Schaffer described him crouching to light his pipe at a campfire:

. . . his swarthy face lighted up by the bright glow, his brass earrings and nail-studded belt catching the glare, with long black plaits of glossy hair and his blanket breeches . . . [52]

It was Sampson Beaver who then gave Schaffer one of the great gifts of her life—a map of how to reach the legendary Maligne Lake, which she had hitherto sought unsuccessfully—thereby repaying his daughter's friend many times over. He drew it from memory of a trip sixteen years earlier, in symbols—"mountains, streams, and passes all included." In 1908 Schaffer, her friend Mollie Adams, "Chief" Warren (her young guide, whom she later married), and "K" Unwin followed the accurate map and became the first white people to document the shores of Chaba Imne (Beaver Lake), ungratefully renamed Maligne for the dangerous river it feeds. In 1911 she returned to survey the lake and its environs, which lie in what is now Jasper National Park.

Mary Sharples Schaffer Warren (1861–1939) was not a Canadian but a Philadelphian, from a wealthy Quaker family. Her father was a businessman and "gentleman farmer," as well as an avid minerologist. She became an amateur naturalist as a child and studied botany as a painter. In 1894 she married Dr. Charles Schaffer, a respected, and much older, doctor whose passion was botany and with whom she worked as an illustrator and photographer until his death in 1903. After completing and publishing his *Alpine Flora of the Canadian Rocky Mountains*, she conquered her fear of horses, bears, and the wilderness, and began her lengthy exploring expeditions, going on horseback with pack train deep into the then mostly uncharted territory for months at a time.

Schaffer's interest in Indians and the West had been awakened when, as a small child, she overheard her cousin Jim, an army officer, telling her parents about the destruction of an Indian village in which women and children were massacred; afterwards he had found a live baby sheltered by the mother's dead body.[53] This story made a profound impression on Mary, and she became obsessed with Indians. In her mid-teens she took her first trip west, met Native people for the first time, and became an inveterate traveler. The Canadian Rockies were her husband's botanical turf, and for the rest of her life Schaffer spent summers on the trails, photographing, writing, and exploring. She finally moved to Banff, and died there.

When Schaffer and Mollie Adams decided to take their plunge into the wilderness, it was unprecedented, and improper, for women to encroach on this steadfastly male territory. As Schaffer recalled,

> . . . there are times when the horizon seems restricted, and we seemed to have reached that horizon, and the limit of all endurance—to sit with folded hands and listen calmly to the stories of the hills we so longed to see, the hills which had lured and beckoned us for years before this long list of men had ever set foot in the country. Our cups splashed over. We looked into each other's eyes and said: "Why not! We can starve as well as they; the muskeg will be no softer for us than for them . . . the waters no deeper to swim, nor the bath colder if we fall in"—so—we planned a trip.[54]

These and many other hardships and exhilarations they did endure, loving almost every minute of it, and documenting their experiences with their (often ineptly hand-colored) photographs of giant peaks, vast rivers, glaciers, and fields of wildflowers. When they were returning from the 1907 expedition, they passed a stranger on the trail near Lake Louise who later described the incident:

> As we drove along the narrow hill road a piebald pack-pony with a china-blue eye came round a bend, followed by two women, black-haired, bare-headed, wearing beadwork squaw jackets and riding straddle. A string of pack-ponies trotted through the pines behind them.
>
> "Indians on the move?" said I. "How characteristic!"
>
> As the women jolted by, one of them very slightly turned her eyes and they were, past any doubt, the comprehending equal eyes of the civilized white woman which moved in that berry-brown face. . . .
>
> The same evening, in a hotel of all the luxuries, a slight woman in a very pretty evening frock was turning over photographs, and the eyes beneath the strictly arranged hair were the eyes of the woman in the beadwork who had quirted the piebald pack-pony past our buggy.[55]

The author of this colonial encounter was, ironically, Rudyard Kipling.

As Levi-Strauss has pointed out, the notion of travel is thoroughly corrupted by power. Mary Schaffer, for all her love of the wilderness (which she constantly called her "playground") was not free from the sense of power that came with being a prosperous "modern" person at "play" in the fields of the conquered. At the same time, she also expressed a very "modern" sense of melancholy and loss as she watched the railroad (which she called a "python") and ensuing "civilization" inching its way into her beloved landscape. More than her photographs, her journals betray a colonial lens. She is condescendingly "fond," but not very respectful, of the "savages" who are often her friends, bemoaning their unpleasantly crude and hard traditional life. In 1911, for instance, her party passed "a Cree village where, when we tried to photograph the untidy spot, the inhabitants scuttled like rabbits to their holes." In 1907, on the same Koontenai Plains where she took the Beavers' portrait, her camp was visited by "old Paul Beaver," presumably a relative of her darling Frances Louise. He eyed their simmering supper "greedily," but

our provisions were reaching that point where it was dangerous to invite any guests, especially Indians, to a meal, so we downed all hospitable inclinations and without a qualm watched him ride away on his handsome buckskin just as darkness was falling.[56]

For all its socially enforced static quality, and for all I've read into it, Mary Schaffer's photograph of Sampson, Leah, and Frances Louise Beaver is "merely" the image of an ephemeral moment. I am first and foremost touched by its peace and freshness. I can feel the ground and grass, warm and damp beneath the people sitting "here" in an Indian summer after disaster had struck, but before almost all was lost. Despite years of critical analysis, seeing is still believing to some extent— as those who control the dominant culture (and those who ban it from Native contexts) know all too well. In works like this one, some of the barriers are down, or invisible, and we have the illusion of seeing for ourselves, the way we never *would* see for ourselves, which is what communication is about.

Notes:

1. Victor Masayesva, in Victor Masayesva and Erin Younger, eds., *Hopi Photographers/Hopi Images* (Tucson: Sun Tracks and University of Arizona Press, 1983), p. 90.

2. Paula Richardson Fleming and Judith Luskey, *The North American Indians in Early Photographs* (New York: Dorset Press, 1988), p. 142.

3. Anonymous, "Our Indian Visitors," *F. Leslie's Illustrated Newspaper* (Denver), June 24, 1871, p. 243.

4. James Baldwin, "A Talk to Teachers" (1963), in Rick Simonson and Scott Walker, eds., *Graywolf Annual Five: Multicultural Literacy* (Saint Paul: Graywolf Press, 1988), p. 8.

5. For the moment, Horace Poolaw (Kiowa) is officially the only "professional" Native photographer on the books, although there were surely others, and the search is on for them. The Eskimo photographer James Manning has mentioned that his grandfather, Peter Pitscolak, was a photographer, and Lee Marmon has also done important local work in Laguna/Acoma. Poolaw (1906–1984) had already bought a small camera and enrolled in a correspondence course in oil coloring when a white landscape photographer named George Long got off the train at Mountain View, Oklahoma, in 1926 and hired him as an apprentice. From then on, he photographed the daily life of the Kiowa. (See Linda Poolaw, *War Bonnets, Tin Lizzies, and Patent Leather Pumps: Kiowa Culture in Transition, 1925–1955* [Stanford: Stanford University Press, 1990], p. 12.)

6. Of the three commercial photographers operating in Albuquerque in 1883, one was a Mrs. E. L. Albright.

7. Jimmie Durham, in *We the People*, New York: Artists Space, 1987, p. 16.

8. Vine Deloria in preface to Christopher Lyman, *The Vanishing Race and Other Illusions* (New York: Pantheon Books, 1982).

9. Masayesva in Masayesva and Younger, *Hopi Photographers*, p. 10.

10. Don Talayesva (with Leo W. Simmons), *Sun Chief* (New Haven: Yale University Press, 1942), p. 252.

11. Masayesva in Masayesva and Younger, *Hopi Photographers*, p. 11.

12. Masayesva in Masayesva and Younger, *Hopi Photographers*, p. 10.

13. Leslie Marmon Silko, *Storyteller* (Boston: Little, Brown and Company, 1981).

14. *Contemporary Native American Photography* (Washington, D.C.: U.S. Department of the Interior/Indian Arts and Crafts Board, 1984).

15. Jean Fredericks in Masayesva and Younger, *Hopi Photographers*, p. 42.

16. William Jenkins in Masayesva and Younger, *Hopi Photographers*, p. 7.

17. Quoted in T. C. McLuhan's introduction to Edward Curtis, *Portraits from North American Indian Life* (n.p.: A & W Visual Library, 1974), p. viii.

18. Curtis, *Portraits*, p. vi.

19. Curtis, *Portraits*, p. x.

20. Curtis, *Portraits*, p. ix.

21. Curtis, *Portraits*, pp. vi–vii.

22. Adolph F. Muhr did his retouching for him. For the record, the anthropologist Franz Boas also retouched his photographs in the name of purism, and John Wesley Powell faked many of his, commissioning his own costumes. (See Linda Scherer, "You Can't Believe Your Eyes: Inaccuracies in Photographs of North American Indians," *Exposure* [Winter, 1978], and Arthur Fox, "Imaginary Indians," *This World* [April 12, 1987], p. 14–15.) The nineteenth-century photographer Ben Wittick sometimes allowed his portrait subjects to choose parts of their regalia from his collection, but also (like most of his contemporaries) chose the costumes and settings himself for commercial appeal, with little regard for cultural accuracy.

23. Lyman, *Vanishing Race*, p. 68.

24. Deloria, preface to Lyman, *Vanishing Race*, n.p.

25. Deloria, preface to Lyman, *Vanishing Race*, n.p.

26. Curtis took his first pictures of Indians in 1898 as "part of the local scenery." A recent exhibition, called "The Lens and the Landscape," is advertised by the portrait of a Native American man.

27. Malek Alloula, *The Colonial Harem* (Minneapolis: University of Minnesota Press, 1986), p. 92.

28. Alloula, *Colonial Harem*, p. 86.

29. Johannes Fabian, *Time and the Other: How Anthropology Makes Its Object* (New York: Columbia University Press, 1983), p. 6.

30. Dean MacCannell, *The Tourist: A New Theory of the Leisure Class* (New York: Schocken Books, 1989), p. 13.

31. William Henry Jackson, *Time Exposure: The Autobiography of William Henry Jackson* (New York: G. P. Putnam's Sons, 1940), pp. 226–28.

32. D. H. Thomas, quoted in T. C. McLuhan, *Dream Tracks: The Railroad and the American Indian, 1890–1930* (New York: Harry N. Abrams, 1985), p. 96.

33. Frederick J. Dockstader in foreword to Patricia Janis Broder, *Shadows on Glass: The Indian World of Ben Wittick* (Savage, Md.: Rowman and Littlefield, 1990), p. 9.

34. L. L. Lyon, "History of Prohibition of Photography of Southwestern Indian Ceremonies," paper presented at the Museum of Natural History, Washington, D.C., April 12, 1986. *Papers of the Archaeological Society of New Mexico*, no. 14, Santa Fe, 1988.

35. The most recent chapter in this struggle for religious privacy is the Hopi Nation's complete ban on outsiders at dances, in response to a portrayal of their sacred Kachinas as incarnations of evil in a comic book.

36. From a photograph by Cradoc Bagshaw, 1975, reproduced in *Handbook of North American Indians*, vol. 9, the Southwest (Washington, D.C.: Smithsonian Institution, 1979), p. 537.

37. See Stephen E. Weil in *The Journal of Art* (2:4, Jan. 1990), p. 26.

38. Alfred M. Bailey, *Field Work of a Museum Naturalist* (Denver: Museum of Natural History, 1971), p. 36.

39. Alloula, *Colonial Harem*, p. 27 (his emphasis).

40. Alloula, *Colonial Harem*, p. 92.

41. Alloula, *Colonial Harem*, p. 64.

42. Alloula, *Colonial Harem*, p. 4.

43. Lyman, *Vanishing Race*, p. 56. Such "dressing up" brought its own bad luck. A famous photograph of Chief Hairy Chin of the Hunkpapa Sioux, dressed in an Uncle Sam costume, was taken by David Barry in 1889, when Hairy Chin led the Fourth of July parade. He died two days later on his return to the Standing Rock reservation, and no other Indian would ever wear the costume.

44. Then there is the reverse situation. I am currently working on an article about "cross-dressing" which will include photographs of Albert Einstein, artist Joseph Beuys, and classical archaeologist Iris Love, among others, all wearing warbonnets.

45. This essay was originally written for *Poetics of Space*, an anthology edited by Steve Yates, forthcoming from the University of New Mexico Press. My thanks to the late Jon Whyte of the Whyte Museum in Banff, author of *Indians in the Rockies* (Banff: Altitude Publishing Ltd., 1985).

46. Johannes Fabian, *Time and the Other*, p. 35.

47. They were Frank Worthington Isham and his wife Mary Rowland, and Rev. Roselle T. Cross and his wife Emma Bridgman. Between them, they spent years in Dakota Territory, Colorado, Wyoming, Nebraska, and Washington.

48. Press release from American Indian Community House, New York City, publicizing a traveling exhibition of Native photographers (see note 14, above).

49. Dennis Grady, "The Devolutionary Image: Toward a Photography of Liberation," *S. F. Camerawork* (16:2–3, Summer/Fall 1989), p. 28.

50. E. J. Hart, ed., *Hunter of Peace: Mary T. S. Schaffer's Old Indian Trails of the Canadian Rockies* (Banff: Whyte Museum, 1980), p. 70.

51. Hart, *Hunter of Peace*, p. 71.

52. Hart, *Hunter of Peace*, p. 72.

53. This sounds like a description of the 1864 massacre of Cheyenne and Arapaho at Sand Creek, in Colorado. A photograph exists of a sad-looking little girl, dressed in elegant European clothes, inaccurately described as the sole survivor of the massacre, later adopted by white people.

54. Hart, *Hunter of Peace*, p. 17.

55. Hart, *Hunter of Peace*, p. 2.

56. Hart, *Hunter of Peace*, p. 69.

Frank Matsura, *Two Girls on Couch*, c. 1910. (Courtesy Okanogan County Historical
Society, Okanogan, Wash.)

Rayna Green

ROSEBUDS OF THE PLATEAU:

Frank Matsura and the Fainting Couch Aesthetic

Two Victorian girls, reclining, like all their sisters, look at us from the Japanese photographer's fainting couch in Okanogan, Washington. Red Rossettis! They might be taking tea with Christina and reading selections from the *Faerie Queene* or William Morris's notes on a new aesthetic for common things. Mrs. Bountiful might be waiting on them for a reading lesson after the weekly meeting of the Browning Society, to introduce them to the higher moral values of Flush the Spaniel and various madwomen in the attic. Maybe some English would-be pornographer lurks in the anteroom, hoping to spank them, or at least to catch a glimpse of their ankles. They're too old for Lewis Carroll, though, and far too dark for Rossetti. They could be from anywhere, brought by ship from Hawaii or Brazil.

I like these girls. I am transfixed by this photo. From the moment I saw it, hanging on the wall, surrounded by other photographs of Indians, contemporaries from the turn of the century, I loved it. There they were, these girls surrounded by Curtis boys dripping dentalia and fur—the sepia kings, shot through spit and petroleum jelly, Lords of the Plains, Potentates of the Potlatch, the Last-Ofs. I take out my immediate distaste on them, but it's Curtis and the other pinhole illusionists I'm after. *Get a life*, I want to say to them. Quit taking out your fantasies on us. Just give me one in overalls and a cowboy hat. Then we can get serious about what was happening to these people.

Enough about Curtis. I don't want to talk about him. You know the rap on him. Then why are we so grateful for his glorious dreams? Every Indian I know has one of them on the wall. Mine came down a long time ago, and now these girls are up there, along with Skeet McAuley's picture of the astroturf Navajo school football field at Golding, Utah.[1] Everyone stops to look at them. Why? Maybe just the glimmer of hostility or frankness, the restrained confrontation in those absolutely Indian faces, the unexpected pose on the couch, these two Victorian Indian girls. I've made up their story. Maybe I don't have to.

The direct, unflinching gaze could turn you into a pillar of salt, into Lot's wife, for having hesitated about who and what they are. *Where* they are is clear enough to nineteenth-century buffs. The flowered couch, the curtains and faded oriental carpet. When I look at it, I smell boiling cabbage. Earl Grey and buttered bread, a boiled egg, a piece of seedcake if you're one of the lucky ones. And that's if Missy has taken a liking to you. Now I know they're servants. The boiling cabbage or the cabbage roses let me in on the secret. They are "tweenies," or kitchen help. Possibly rented out by the Presbyterian School for Indian Girls to Mrs. Gotrocks, wife of the town copper baron, patroness of the church and of redskins who can be saved through hard work.

How did Frank Matsura get them into the studio and onto the couch? Maybe Mrs. Gotrocks or maybe the headmistress of the minister of the prison-like school forced them to go. Maybe someone thought it was funny to get these servant girls, these too-old schoolgirls, these Indians in Victorian sheep's clothing, to pose like all the Golden Girls. It is funny, after all. These girls don't belong here. They're pretenders, aren't they? Juxtaposition and contradiction do make for comedy. It's the unexpected. But it's only unexpected because of that damned Curtis who won't let me stop talking about him. Because of him and the magic-box boys, our eyes have been wrenched from command of our own realities, even when "art" was what we or they were after.

These girls don't think it's funny, and not because they're being taken advantage of. No soul stealing going on here. They appear fairly comfortable, maybe a bit stiff. They're friends, maybe sisters or cousins. Salish probably, maybe from Colville. Matsura was everywhere in that area, and there's nothing to suggest where they came from. Just out there somewhere. If they'd had "typical" outfits on, we'd think them co-wives of some unregenerate Native polygamist. Maybe they were just that, and the preachers took them away from the savages to save their souls. If that's the case, they didn't get far. These ladies are unregenerate.

One of them has clearly bought it more than the other. Look at her, with bows in her hair and bows on her shoes. She's the one holding the silk roses—those roses again. She makes me feel as though there ought to be a verse below, of the "blooms-there-the-flower-that-may-wither-and-die" variety. Except that withering flower is not for her, but for her people who've just been locked up on the rez forever, allotted out, potlatched out, poxed out, sung out, drummed out. For now, though, she lies on the couch holding those damned roses as if there were no yesterday. Her slight smile is faintly encouraging, just a little hesitant, and a lot vulnerable—maybe loved to death. For me it's not phony. She can deal with this couch, the white dress and roses, the studio and the photographer. She knows it's just a role, but I think she likes it, accepts it, the Victorian girl bit. She still believes things might turn out okay.

The other woman is a different story. She's had it rougher. Maybe the mister in the house where she's a servant has had a go at her. Or she doesn't trust Frank, even though he looks just like some of her people. Or she likes her friend and Frank well enough to pose, but she doesn't buy it, thinks it's for white girls and knows better for herself. She gives it her best, looking right into the camera. But the situation remains a little confrontational. "Come on down." "Make my day." "I ain't afraid of nothin'." She's the kind that would give you a hard time, a real rez girl already. The look and the head-rag say it all. "Put me in these clothes and shoes. Lay me down on the fainting couch, but I won't slump gracefully and call for my salts. I've seen everything I need to see and more. I'm comfortable, whatever you think." If she lived today she'd wear jeans, shades, and a punky black T-shirt. She'd be wearing the purple shawl at the powwow and the other girl would be at mass every Sunday.

Still, the picture gets them clear, if not right. No dress-up in trad-rags, no foo-foo, no pretense, no spit and vaseline on the lens. This is them, then, in that condition, in that place. They lived, worked, or went to school in places that looked like this studio. Maybe it was anti-Romanticism, anti-Curtis, anti-Catlin on Matsura's part to keep them in "merikano" clothes. But it's also possible that he was trying to civilize them, Americanize them, just as the government did. Maybe he took away their Indian clothes, their fish, their songs, just like the government and the Christians wanted. Maybe *he* wanted them to be Victorian girls. But wouldn't he have chosen whiter, lighter, mixed-blood girls? Perhaps not, if the idea was to get the "real ones" that the sexual conquest of North America had missed so far. And while we're at it, isn't it strange that people thought miscegenation was a great way to go with Indians but didn't think so much of it for black folks? A look at the politics of skin and civilization is not irrelevant here.

I really want to take Matsura and the girls at "face" value, but I'm trying to puzzle out a hidden or deeper message in this picture. Part of me is simply grateful for its lack of surface trickery, and that grateful part makes me reluctant to pick it apart. I hate the way I keep doubting Matsura and his motives, but then, there's been so little to inspire faith. Complicated, isn't it? As Native people, we're grateful for the romantic "before" portraits of what we were like when the bad guys came and mucked it all up, and then we feel worse when we learn how badly they've tricked us, given us illusions, dreams of a past we can't get back. The Age of the Golden Tipi. Then we also hate these "after" pictures where they've made us just like them.

Still, don't you like the ladies in this photograph? Maybe they saved up their wages and came on down because they wanted their pictures. You can tell they were living through whatever it was they had to live through. Maybe they ran away from Mrs. Gotrocks' house, or from the Indian school, like my grandma did. Or maybe they stayed for a lifetime. Someone up there at Colville or wherever could tell me who they were and what happened to them. I hope their children and grandchildren know about this picture. *Grandma was a pistol!* I'd say to them.

These girls don't make me feel ashamed. Not like the pictures from the art class at Hampton Institute where the ones in Victorian dresses and suits painted the savage in his savage outfit. And not like the double-take Catlin painting where the Noble Savage on one side wears his feathers, and on the other side struts drunkenly in a para-white-boy morning coat and top hat. Maybe I'm just glad Matsura photographed Indian women doing anything aside from making pots, tatting up baskets, or chewing hides. These ladies have got no small measure of bravado. And not the "It's-a-good-day-to-die" kind. I appreciate that often necessary and brave machismo, given the circumstances, but there might have been other ways of weathering the storm. These girls have got it. Matsura saw it. What's more, he took its picture.

And what can we say about Frank Matsura? His story is as almost as vague as that of the girls in the picture. JoAnn Roe, the only person who's tried to investigate his life, and wrote a book about him, still knows very little.[2] Everyone in Okanogan who knew him the ten years he was there seems to have liked what they knew. But nobody knows if he was the Sakae Matsura who applied for a U.S. passport in 1901, arriving at Conconully, Washington, in 1903. The Frank Matsura we know got a job as a cook's helper and laundryman at the Hotel Elliott, taking pictures madly in his spare time. Eventually he opened a photographic studio where he sold Oriental curios and postcards made from his own photographs.

Maybe he was the aristocratic Sakae Matsura. He appeared to have some money. He owned a samurai sword, was well educated, and spoke excellent English. Maybe he was married in Japan. Maybe he was a newspaperman or an entertainer. He was a social extrovert and liked parties. He kept a huge garden, sending flowers to the ill. He was, according to all reports, deeply respectful of women and "circumspect in his relationships with them," inviting some to have tea with him as long as they were accompanied by an appropriate chaperone. He wrote an article for the local newspaper on the education of Japanese women, quoting John Stuart Mill on the importance of individuality. His best friend, William Compton Brown, was a young lawyer (later a judge) who wrote a book about Indian treaties, *The Indian Side of the Story*. To him fell Matsura's plates and films after his sudden death from tuberculosis in 1913.

Matsura photographed everything in this town and region, including the first panoramic views of Okanogan. He took pictures of the miners, cowboys, homesteaders, ships and riverboats, the irrigation projects and engineers, the orchards and ranches, the schoolchildren, taverns, and drunks of the region. Some were used in Great Northern Railway advertising and shown in expositions. He made funny photos as well, of himself and his friends clowning around in Indian blankets, clown costumes, and baby bonnets. And of course he took pictures of Indians: Colvilles, Salish of all sorts, Nez Percé with their Palousey (Appaloosa) horses. They came to his studio dressed in their best, along with the other townspeople. When he died, they buried him overlooking the valley and hills of Colville. The *Okanogan Independent* reported:

A shadow of sorrow was cast over the community . . . by the sudden death of . . . the Japanese photographer who has been a part and parcel of the city . . . unpretentious, unassuming, modest. . . . He was a photographer of fine ability. . . . He was always on the job. Whenever anything happened Frank was there with his camera to record the event. . . . He has done more to advertise Okanogan city and valley than any other individual.

Matsura's photographs of Indians certainly span a wider range of types and scenes than those of other better-known photographers of the time. His images of Indian ranchers and cowboys alone give us a better sense of what and who Indians were during those awful years after reservationization. Everybody writes about the old warriors with nothing to do but join the Wild West Show, and God knows we've got lots of pictures of these guys. But here, in Matsura's *oeuvre*, are the real cowboys—Paul Timentwa, Joe Louie, Joe Thomas, Paul Antoine, and Johnnie Poynton, the Colville medicine man/cowboy. They're riding horses, playing cards, dashing off on posses with the sheriff, wearing those delicious angora chaps, beaded gloves, silk neckerchiefs, bear coats, and broad-brimmed hats.

But Matsura shot more than the dandies and the bully boys. He also photographed summer tipi settlements, families wearing their traditional and American-style clothing, Minnie McDonald, the beautiful Colville horsewoman (and horse thief), and little fat laughing children in cradleboards and calico sacks. When Indians wore ceremonial and traditional clothing, it was theirs, not something fancy and inappropriate that Matsura had dragged up out of his trunk for the photographic moment. That's why I trust that his picture of these girls wasn't a joke, all tricked up to make us think "How absurd!"

Maybe I trust Matsura because he was an outsider, a foreigner. Indians weren't even a social category for him until he got to Washington. Friends reported that Frank and Moses George, a Colville, used to joke about their mutual inability to say the letter *L*. Maybe he knew a little about how these Indians felt. Although well liked, he was still a "little Japanese" at a time of great American prejudice and violence against Asians. What he shows of Indians, however, what he shows of this frontier world, is not deviance and heartbreak and isolation. There is a rather startling integration of himself, of Indians, of others who might have been strange and alien and enemies elsewhere. Matsura's Okanogan world cheers the hell out of me. Yes, the land settlements were a mess, and yes, the homesteaders and the Army Corps of Engineers and the lumber mills and fruit companies took it all. But somewhere, in this world he shows us, Indians aren't weird, heartbroken exiles, or zoo animals for the expositions, endangered species preserved forever in photographic gelatin. Like those girls on the fainting couch, they are changed, but in control.

Maybe I just want it be that way, even for one brief, glorious moment. Maybe it's exactly what I want for all of us. How will I and my friends be shown—as mixed-bloods who've lost it, our briefcases clutched anxiously to our sides, our three-piece suits ill-fitting and never right? Or, worse, with our ceremonial clothes looking like we got them from some German hobbyist in the Schwarzwald. Maybe these girls calm my fears. Generations survived after them because they were tough, flexible, sound. Matsura saw it. He wasn't a death-bringer, an undertaker for the Indian past, a necrophiliac who wanted to photograph the "last of" anything.

This magic-box has been a real problem, as a tool of art, because we all thought it saw reality, the "truth." It's gotten between us and the truth about Indians, that's for sure. Good, somehow, for this "little Japanese" photographer to have gotten through the muck to see the possibilities. We don't have to make up his story; it's there in his vision. I hope those girls will forgive me for making up their stories, for using them to comment on my own fears and passions. The little Oklahoma Indian girl that was me, who was made to feel incredibly deviant for reading English novels, found something healing in the sight of those girls on the fainting couch. They could have been my grandma when she was young. The little girl in overalls who rode horses and sang "Amazing Grace" in Cherokee felt better upon seeing their shirtwaists and bows, just like the ones my relatives wore at the Cherokee Female Seminary.

"One set of people in overalls dispossessing another set of people in overalls" is what a historian friend calls Removal and the loss of Indian Territory. Let the dreamers howl at the missing feathers. The ladies at the Cherokee Female Seminary, true to their Victorian sensibilities, called their school newspaper *A Wreath of Cherokee Rosebuds*. These "Plateau rosebuds" on the fainting couch in Frank Matsura's photograph remind us that Indian survival was more complex and diverse than most pictures of it would have us imagine.

Notes:

1. Skeet McAuley, *Sign Language* (New York: Aperture Press, 1989).
2. JoAnn Roe, *Frank Matsura: Frontier Photographer* (Seattle: Madrona Publishers, 1981).

Walter Ferguson (?), *Geronimo at the Wheel*, 1904. (Courtesy National Archives, Washington D.C., 75-1C-1.) The picture was taken at the 101 Ranch near Ponca City, Oklahoma, while the Apache leader was a prisoner of war at Fort Sill. He was given special permission to visit the ranch for a meeting of the National Editorial Association. He died in 1909 and was buried on the reservation at Fort Sill. The label on this photograph asserts: "He is generally accredited with being the most bloodthirsty Indian warrior of all time."

Jimmie Durham

GERONIMO!

The American myths about who the Apaches are, and who Geronimo was, involve such well-worn clichés that it is difficult to re-address the reality. Schoolboys and military men are taught to yell "Geronimo!" when they jump into the swimming pool or into battle. So at least we can begin by asking why that is. Why don't those children yell some other name? They do not *admire* Geronimo or the Apaches. In the American myth, Apaches are a symbol of inscrutable cruelty. Is Geronimo's name invoked because he evokes American fear—a fear that has been "conquered"? If so, then the fearsome "object" has obviously not been "conquered" at all.

Having begun with a question I cannot answer, I now come to a different but intimately related level of reality. Today, Geronimo's family, his descendents, are leaders of an Apache reservation that is still hard-pressed from all sides, forced to expend resources and energy simply to fight more colonial incursions. We must recognize that Geronimo and his people are not defeated, and that these days are still part of an urgent and desperate situation that demands active solidarity.

Why are you looking at these photos? What do you expect to learn? What do you expect to feel? What do you expect to happen next?

And what am I doing? What do I expect?

I am faced with my usual dilemma. On the one hand, how can I write, carry on intellectual or cultural investigations, when our situations demand activism? And on the other hand, to whom might I address my investigations? How and why can I assume a basic trust in an untrustworthy situation? Am I creating neurotic complexities because of my own confusions and guilt? Am I even needlessly inserting myself in a short essay about a photo of someone else, and so using Geronimo to further my own career?

55

Reader, as you read, I want you to have similar doubts and recognize a similar need for activism, at a time and in circumstances that should be intolerable to all of us.

In American morality, integrity and intellectual clarity are constantly stifled by a refusal to acknowledge the colonial nature of American nations, followed by the refusal to acknowledge the predicaments and rights of colonized peoples. Is it really possible to take over someone's house, murder most of the family, lock the remaining victims in the closet, and then pretend that it is your own little house on the prairie in the suburbs?

All photographs of American Indians are photographs of dead people, in that their *use* assumes ownership of the subject, which is seen as static, completely "understandable." Except, of course, even the tightest system is not completely closed. Geronimo, as an Indian "photographic subject," blew out the windows. On his own, he reinvented the concept of photographs of American Indians. At least he did so as far as he could, concerning pictures of himself, which are so ubiquitous that he must have sought "photo opportunities" as eagerly as the photographers. Yet even when he was "posed" by the man behind the camera, he seems to have destroyed the pose and created his own stance. In every image, he looks through the camera at the viewer, seriously, intently, with a specific message. Geronimo uses the photograph to "get at" those people who imagine themselves as the "audience" of his struggles. He seems to be trying to see us. He is demanding to be seen, on his own terms.

Perhaps that is why his (Spanish) name is so often invoked. Geronimo established his own "view" of himself in the American consciousness, so that he could not so easily be "pinned down." But also, his people were forced into war with the U.S. (and with Mexico) just at the time when the U.S. was hoping to become nostalgic about its wars against American Indians. The "Vanishing Redman" was already being promoted.

We should remember, however, that violent persecution had been the lot of the Apaches for a couple of hundred years before those wars of the 1880s and '90s. Geronimo had to have recognized that the tragedies of his life—seeing most of his family murdered—were part of an ongoing atrocity perpetrated by Spanish and then U.S. colonists for generations.

I am going to derail the train here for a moment to answer the "expert-on-Indians" I hear screaming over my sentences. You are saying, Señor Expert, that the Apaches were bad guys to other Indians, that they raided pueblo villages, etc. That argument is slimy and immoral. It might have some validity if the colonists had at any time (including now, with the false fight between Hopi and Navajo at Big Mountain) defended any Indian community under any circumstances. The fact that England is still colonizing a part of Ireland does not give me, as a third party, the right to decimate England.

Geronimo had the right to be hopeless and crazy, to be reduced to a passive beggar like so many Indian people at the time. Yet even when he was finally captured, he reportedly said, "So you have captured me; the Mexicans would have killed me." And then he looks at the camera, at the "audience," and tells us that he will continue to resist.

Many people are surprised at the photograph we are contemplating here. It has not been as widely published as other photos of Geronimo, and many assume that he was killed in battle or died of a "broken heart" in a Florida prison. This photo does not fit the myth that the U.S. must continually rebuild. Sometimes Indian people are ashamed, or at least embarrassed by it, as though Geronimo were caught being a foolish old man.

We do not want to see the valiant and "savage" old warrior in a top hat, as though he had given up and accepted "civilization." We do not want to see him in this century. We want him to remain in the (designated) past. Such reactions remind me of a silly "B.C." comic strip in which a character discovers that clams have legs. "Clams got legs!" he screams hysterically. So "Geronimo can drive a car!"

My copy of this photo is from an unidentified book. (Little in life arrives from pure sources; so much the better.) The text below it explains that Geronimo "obtained pocket money through the sale of photographs of himself . . ."* *Pocket* money. As though the writer imagines Geronimo as a child wanting to buy ice cream. But it was this century, and Geronimo was old. He had no "job" (and no home). He needed money.

Reader, although I hope, of course, that these words about the vision and resistance of a great leader might serve in some small way as a constructive act, I am in fact selling them—because I need pocket money. We are seldom offered "bank" money.

Do you speak a second language? Geronimo spoke at least three: his own, English and Spanish. He was also a strategist and a resistance leader. We can imagine that in 1905 he had his wits about him, and understood more of your culture than you would have understood of his. In this photo he does much more than present his existence in the face of attempts to "disappear" him. But, as usual, he is not *asking* for anything—not even "understanding." Instead, a part of his message here is, as always, a *demand* to be recognized.

In early photos Geronimo is so beautifully and belligerently at home in the chaparral, and he almost always has his rifle ready. (I hope he took that rifle from a soldier, but he could just as well have dressed up as a *vaquero* and bought it in a store.) Later, in the twentieth century, when he is not allowed a rifle or his chaparral, he puts on your hat, takes the wheel, and stares the camera down. This photo makes clear that no matter what had been taken from him, he had given up nothing. This photo is exactly like earlier photos of Geronimo, when he was obviously at war. If Geronimo had been defeated, he would have stayed on the reservation, dressed "properly" for America's Indian myths.

Geronimo is messing with established reality here. The guy next to him is "doing the right thing," with his noble pose, his Plains headdress and pipe bag. Another guy, in the back seat, is doing "youthful bravado." Geronimo's action, his stance, is a brilliant intervention. Look at his face getting in your face. He continues to resist, to *maintain*, through changes. Look closely at the other guys. He is solidly and deliberately *set*, in a posture that seems to be attempting to project words, thoughts, at us, instead of known symbols. He is trying to photograph himself, but from within. He is taking a photograph of his thoughts.

It is as though he was using his personal integrity, no matter what the situation, to reach, to challenge our own personal integrity. That implied a profound trust. He was not saying, "I am a human being"; he was saying, "I know *you* are human beings . . ."

Editor's note:
*The caption appeared in *Fighting Indians of the West*, by Martin F. Schmidt and Dee Brown (New York: Charles Scribners & Sons, 1948).

Jaune Quick-To-See Smith

FAMILY ALBUM

My father's great aunt, Emma Harriet Minesinger Waymack Magee, was born on January 8, 1866, to a white father and a Shoshone/Flathead mother—Nellie Quick-To-See Minesinger (1826–1932). The photograph of Emma in traditional dress and braids was probably taken in the 1880s. The dress is called a cut-wing and is patterned after deerskin clothing. When the white traders arrived in the Bitterroot Valley in Montana, some time in the 1850s, calico became a popular trade item with the Indians. Emma's dress has attached sleeves of a separate calico pattern, which is still popular today. She was an avid beadworker, so she probably made her belt as well as the rest of her outfit. My cousin Jerry Slater stayed with Aunt Emma when he was in grade school. He told me that she beaded all the time, smoked her pipe, and bossed everybody around.

When Emma was born, the Jesuits, trappers, and traders had only recently arrived on the Flathead. (They came late to this remote area with an unwelcoming climate; in fact, the real death knell for us wasn't sounded until the 1930s, when the settlers built irrigation ditches that made farming possible, and the rest of the land was grabbed.) Life was full of turmoil for all our families as changes came in rapid succession. In 1890, the remaining members of our tribe were removed at gunpoint by U.S. Cavalry soldiers from the Bitterroot Valley—which had been our homeland for well over ten thousand years—to our present-day reservation about two hundred miles to the north. By then, the Jesuits had a firm grip on our families. Teaching people to read and write was only incidental to their larger mission. Wholesale indoctrination into Christianity was part of a militaristic and culturally destructive program. Among the interesting "artifacts" from this era of whitewashed Indians are the braids cut off and banned by the priests; some are now found in museums. If the men managed to retrieve their braids, they hid them so that they could pin them on for dancing or ceremonies which had to take place in secret.

Emma Waymack Magee, second from right in the front row. To her left, in beaded gauntlets, is Nellie Monteray Minesinger. (Courtesy Grace Patterson McComas.)

Emma Magee at Thirty, 1896. (Courtesy *Montana Farmer-Stockman*.)

Emma Magee as a Young Lady, in front of the George White House, Hellgate, Mont. (Courtesy Mr. and Mrs. Clarence White, Missoula, Mont.)

Arthur Albert Smith, c. 1919. (Courtesy Jaune Quick-To-See Smith.)

The second picture of Emma Magee was taken in her thirtieth year, 1896. She has now taken on "civilized" dress and hairstyle. You would never know that she was a woman who knew where to dig bitterroot, who made her own moccasins, beaded, and spoke Salish. Whereas the earlier picture was a snapshot, this one is a studio portrait. (In all of her pictures, Emma showed only her left profile. When she was five years old her brother, who was shooting bumble bees with a bow and arrow, accidentally hit her in the right eye and blinded her.)

By this time, Emma was probably working as a maidservant for a white family. This was standard operating procedure. The priests not only indoctrinated the children, but further advanced their assimilation program by farming out their "converts" as young adults to work as day laborer and servants for white families. If the Jesuits were successful, their students would marry white and continue the cultural destruction. But in those times, men who married Indian women were called "Squawmen"; they often took on the cultural attributes of the Indian people when the women chose to revert to traditional ways.

In another photograph, Emma is seated in a group with her son Peter,[1] her two brothers—John and Henry Minesinger—their mixed blood children, and her mother, Nellie Quick-To-See, whose name I took when I was in my early twenties. Although they are all dressed in white people's clothing, Nellie proudly displays her beaded gauntlets which I'm sure she made herself. Emma recalled that Nellie taught her two daughters "beadwork, embroidery, knitting, sewing and cooking. From buckskin we made gloves, moccasins, and suits. Buckskin was sewed with deer sinews. Other sewing was done with either white or black thread, which we bought in skeins. How novel the first thread on spools seemed to us."[2]

In the 1890s—and on into the 1960s—open displays of Indian culture were frowned upon by the priest and white people in the vicinity. My older brothers and sisters have told me that our grandmother would powder their faces and arms with white flour before going to town, to lessen white prejudice. The only way to survive was to act white, dress white, and think Indian secretly in your head and your heart. My father, who was very dark and couldn't "pass," taught me this lesson at an early age.

The cowboy dandy in the fourth photograph is my father, Arthur Albert Smith. It was taken around 1918 or 1920, when he was about eighteen. Posed stiffly, with arms suspended in awkward affectation, he waits for the photographer to signal that it's okay to move. It looks as though there's mud on his shoes and chaps, so I suspect he had ridden into town on his horse in his working clothes and was stopped by an itinerant photographer. That railing he's supposedly perched on could be a stool in front of a painted backdrop. (Photographers commonly traveled with window-shade scenery.)

Arthur Smith was born in 1901 at the Métis colony at Pincher Creek, Alberta, Canada. His father, whose Indian mother had been purchased for fifty dollars, was

Métis (Cree and French). My father was raised on the Flathead Reservation by his great-grandmother Nellie Quick-To-See Minesinger, his great-aunt Emma Magee, and his grandmother, Mary Minesinger Miles. He was raised by these three women "in the old ways," as they say at home. He was sent to the Jesuit school at St. Ignatius but escaped repeatedly to return to his grandmother's. According to family stories, the women spoiled him and allowed him to do whatever he pleased. He told me he could ride a horse before he could walk. Horses were his first love throughout his life. At an early age he discovered he could earn money by rounding up wild horses off the white farmers' land, breaking them to ride, and selling them back to the whites.

Life on the Flathead was chaotic and unsettling when my father was growing up. Whites were grabbing land and resources at an ever-increasing rate and pushing the Indians aside. My father lived his whole life with prejudice. A horse trader himself, and noted for his knowledge of horses, he came from a long line of traders, most of whom spoke several languages. Since he was raised with traditional ways, it is likely that he spoke more than Salish—probably some Kootenai and Shoshone too. I see my father in *The Surrounded*, an autobiographical novel by the Flathead writer D'Arcy McNickle, which gives an accurate account of life on the reservation in the 1930s. It was a split world, a world of fading good and looming evil.

All this is invisible in the young man's picture, which suggests a gentle strength and a good-natured outlook that promises a bright future. Between the binges of alcoholism and violence that plagued him all his life, my father was a gentle, kind, and giving person who cared about other humans and all animals. There's a youthful cockiness in the tipped hat and "cowboy" pose, as well as a fresh-faced naïveté. My father was attractive to Indian and white women. By the time he was fifteen, he was married to a Kootenai woman; he was to have five more recorded marriages.

Portraits are deceptive because of what they don't tell. Captured in one moment of time, we can contemplate what the subject is doing or thinking, or even guess about their lives, but the difficulty with these Indian portraits is that often what they show us is just not the way it was. Although I've listened to white people tell about photographs of their grandmother or their father with dreamy stories and a certain reverence in their voices, my own feelings about these pictures are painful. I remember all too well the trauma I suffered when a white sheriff would come in the middle of the night to take my father away because they were looking for a "hot" saddle, and "you know you can't trust them." Even though his reputation for honesty was impeccable, he was Indian, and that made him suspect. I felt pain for the unspoken—the things my father didn't name, recite, or refute. I felt he was a dignified victim in a malevolent society that was lacking in passion and humanity. Sometimes I think that he was born one hundred years too late.

Trading was not only in my family's blood, but also in my tribe's. We were the easternmost group of the Salish speakers. We formed a human chain of traders extending to the Pacific and up the coast. We traded and hunted with tribes north into Canada and we traded and fished with "River Indians" from the west. Fish oil, dried salmon, berries, root, and shell were exchanged for buffalo goods such as robes and jerky from the Plains. We were acknowledged as accommodating, generous, and particularly honest by other tribes and by whites too.

My cousin Gerald Slater and I follow this tradition in our own ways. He's a founder of Salish-Kootenai College and of the Two Eagles School (an alternative high school for Indian students kicked out of public school, or confined to detention centers). My activism—organizing Indian exhibitions, seeking out, advising, and supporting young Indian artists—is another extension of our trading legacy. Jerry and I "trade" and network information and systems rather than material goods.

Although, as a tribe, the Flathead were greatly influenced by white culture, I believe one of our most effective survival tactics has been our maneuverability between two worlds. Our strength—and that of our tribe—comes from thousands of years of being "bridges" between cultures, and we continue today in this unique position.

Notes:

1. Emma Waymack Magee lost her first two children to a house fire in Thompson Falls, Montana, in July 1887. Later a third child, abandoned by her then estranged husband, disappeared without a trace. Eight years later, her fourth child—Peter, pictured here—died of Rocky Mountain Spotted Fever, and just after that the lost child was found. He died in the Philippines in 1920. Her only surviving child, a daughter named Hazel, from her second marriage, graduated from the Sherman Indian School at Riverside, California, and attended business college.

2. *Mountain Memories: The Life of Emma Magee in the Rocky Mountain West, 1866–1950*, edited by Ida S. Patterson (Pablo, Montana: Salish Kootenai Community College, 1981), p. 37. In 1940 Emma moved to California to live briefly with her daughter's family. Homesick, she returned to St. Ignatius on the Flathead reservation, where she died in 1950. Emma Magee ended her memoirs, at a time when "time's relentless hand has penciled my brown-skinned face with many tiny furrows":
Sitting beside my window, I often look up to the changeless Mission Mountains. At this southern extremity the loftiest peaks of the range rise boldly against the blue. Here within the shadow of these colossal stone monuments of immortality, I am content to spend the sunset of my life.

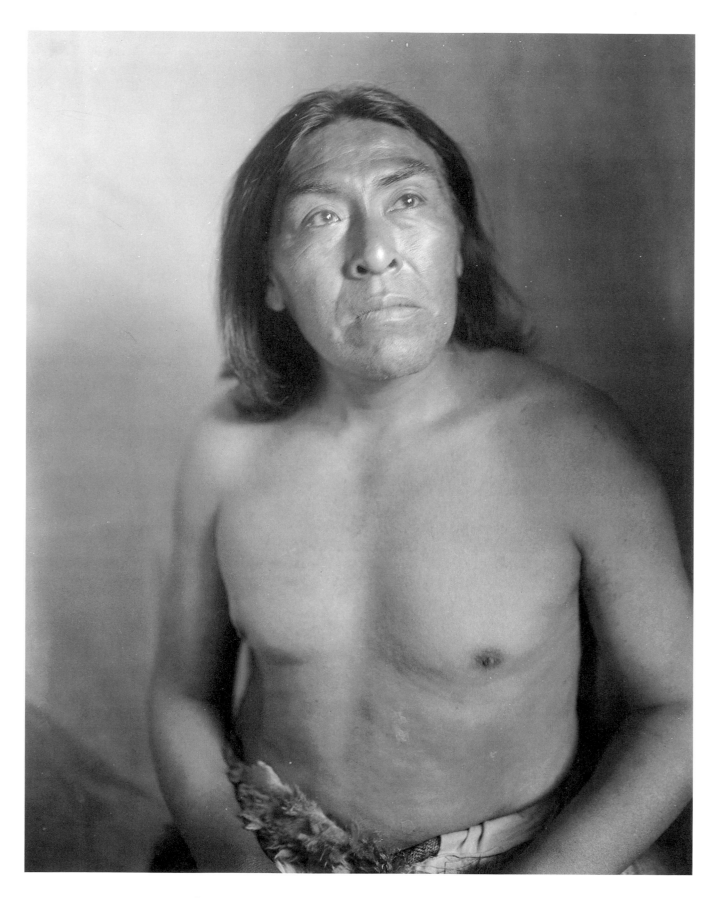

Joseph Dixon (Rodman Wanamaker Expedition), *Ishi*. (Courtesy Department of
Library Services, American Museum of Natural History, New York, 317047.)

Gerald Vizenor

ISHI BARES HIS CHEST:
Tribal Simulations and Survivance

Ishi is not his real name. He posed in this photograph, a backlighted simulation, and this is not that tribal man captured three generations ago in a slaughterhouse in northern California. He was thin and wore a canvas shirt then, a natural philosopher and lonesome hunter, not the image of the stout wild man lost and found with a bare chest who stared over the camera.

He is not the last man of stone. He is not the obscure other, the mortal evidence of savagism, or the last crude measure of uncivilization in the dead voices of racial photographs. He came out of the mountains in an undershirt; later he was redressed at the museum, and then told to bare his chest for the curious photographers.

Ishi told stories to be heard not remembered and with a sense of time that would never be released in a museum. Overnight he became the everlasting unknown, the man who would never vanish in the cruel ironies of civilization.

Ishi was given a watch "which he wore and kept wound but not set," wrote Theodora Kroeber in *Ishi in Two Worlds* (Berkeley: University of California Press, 1965). He understood time by the sun and other means; his "watch was an article of pride and beauty to be worn with chain and pendant, not a thing of utility."

This tribal survivor evaded the barbarians, summer tourists, and the unnatural miners in search of precious minerals; now, as a captured portrait, he endures the remembrance of their romantic heirs. The gaze of those behind the camera haunts the unseen margins of the photograph; the obscure presence of witnesses at the simulation of savagism could become the last epiphanies of a chemical civilization.

He was asked to start a fire in the natural way, and he showed his admirers how to hunt with various bows and arrows. He heard the rush of mountain water, the wind over stone, and told bear stories, but he could have told even more about the violence of civilization. The miners were the real savages; they had no books, no manners, no natural touch, no museums, no stories in the blood, and their harsh breath poisoned the seasons.

Ishi came out of the mountains and was invited to a cultural striptease and the centerfold of manifest manners and histories; he crossed the scratch line of savagism and civilization with one name, and outlived the photographers. His survivance, that sense of mediation in tribal stories, is heard in a word that means "one of the people," and that word became his name. So much the better, and he never told the anthropologists, reporters, and curious practitioners his sacred tribal name, not even his nicknames. He might have said, "The ghosts were generous in the museum, and now these men pretend to know me in their name."

"He was the last of his tribe," wrote Mary Ashe Miller in the *San Francisco Call* (September 6, 1911). He "feared people" and "wandered, alone, like a hunted animal. . . . The man is as aboriginal in his mode of life as though he inhabited the heart of an African jungle, all of his methods are those of primitive peoples."

Ishi became the unheard survivor, the wild other to those he trusted in silence. The notion of the aboriginal and the primitive combined both racialism and postmodern speciesism, a linear consideration that was based on the absence of monotheism, civilization, institutional violence, and written words, more than on the presence of imagination, oral stories, and actual behavior.

Miller wrote that hunting "has been his only means of living and that has been done with bow and arrow of his own manufacture, and with snares. Probably no more interesting individual could be found today than this nameless Indian."

Ishi smiled, shrugged his shoulders, and looked past the camera. The witnesses and nervous photographers, he might have wondered, were lost and lonesome in their own technical activities. Whatever they valued in the creation of the other they had lost in the casual narratives of their own lives.

Susan Sontag wrote in *On Photography* (New York: Farrar, Straus and Giroux, 1978) that photographs are "experience captured, and the camera is the ideal arm of consciousness in its acquisitive mood." The camera captures others, not the experiences of the photographer; the presence of the other is discovered in a single shot, the material reduction of a pose, and invented in a collection of pictures.

The tribes have become the better others, to be sure, and the closer the captured experiences are to the last wild instances in the world, the more valuable are the photographs. Nothing, of course, was ever last that can be seen in a picture. The camera creates an instance that never existed in tribal stories; the last and lost was not in tribal poses but in the remembrance of the witness who dies behind the camera. To be heard was once a course of survivance in tribal imagination; now, however, the tribes must prove with photographs the right to be seen and heard as the other. Mere presence is never the last word at the borders and margins of civilization; the sounds of stories, human touch, and visions must be documented with photographs. Simulations are the outset and bear our tribal presence at the borders.

Sontag argues that "there is something predatory in the act of taking a picture. To photograph people is to violate them, by seeing them as they never see themselves, by having knowledge of them they can never have; it turns people into objects that can be symbolically possessed."

The tribes are sealed, not real, in photographs; these simulations are the casual narratives of museum consciousness, the remorse of civilization. Tribal stories, on the other hand, are mediations, and more is heard and seen in oral stories than in a collection of pictures.

"The primitive notion of the efficacy of images presumes that images possess the qualities of real things," wrote Sontag, "but our inclination is to attribute to real things the qualities of an image."

Ishi told an interpreter, "I will live like the white people from now on." The Bureau of Indian Affairs had promised him protection but he would remain with his friends in the museum. "I want to stay where I am, I will grow old here, and die in this house."

Alfred Kroeber, the anthropologist who cared for Ishi, wrote that "he never swerved from his first declaration." He lived and worked in the museum. "His one great dread, which he overcame but slowly, was of crowds." Ishi said "*hansi saltu*" when he saw the ocean and the crowded beach for the first time. The words were translated as "many white people."

Ishi was captured and possessed forever by the camera, not by agencies of a wild government. The sheriff secured a "pathetic figure crouched upon the floor," the *Oroville Register* reported on August 29, 1911. "The canvas from which his outer shirt was made had been roughly sewed together. His undershirt had evidently been stolen in a raid upon some cabin. His feet were almost as wide as they were long, showing plainly that he had never worn either moccasins or shoes. In his ears were rings made of buckskin thongs."

Kroeber pointed out that "he has perceptive powers far keener than those of highly educated white men. He reasons well, grasps an idea quickly, has a keen sense of humor, is gentle, thoughtful, and courteous and has a higher type of mentality than most Indians." Thomas Waterman administered psychological tests and concluded in a newspaper interview that "this wild man has a better head on him than a good many college men." (Berkeley: *Ishi, The Last Yahi: A Documentary History*, Robert Heizer and Theodora Kroeber, eds., 1979.)

These college men, however, were the same men who discovered and then invented an outsider, the last of his tribe, with their considerable influence and power of communication. They were not insensitive, to be sure, but their museums would contribute to the simulations of savagism. At the same time some of these educated men were liberal nihilists, and their academic strategies dispraised civilization. Ishi trusted his new world, and those who honored him were bettered in their careers. He had been liberated from violence and starvation in the mountains; a wild transformation from the silhouette of the hunted to the heuristic pleasures of a museum.

Theodora Kroeber wrote that he "put on weight rapidly after coming within reach of the fleshpots of civilization and their three times a day recurrence. In a couple of months he had gained between forty and fifty pounds."

Sheriff Webber "removed the cartridges from his revolver" and "gave the weapon to the Indian. The aborigine showed no evidence that he knew anything regarding its use. A cigarette was offered to him, and while it was very evident that he knew what tobacco was, he had never smoked it in that form, and had to be taught the art."

At the University of California a week later, "the unknown refused to obey orders" for the first time. "He was to be photographed in a garment of skins, and when the dressing for the aboriginal part began he refused to remove his overalls," reported Mary Ashe Miller. "He say he not see any other people go without them," said the tribal translator, Sam Batwi, "and he say he never take them off no more."

Miller wrote that the "battery of half a dozen cameras focused upon him was a new experience and evidently a somewhat terrifying one. He stood with his head back and a half smile on his face, but his compressed lips and dilated nostrils showed that he was far from happy. . . . His name, if he knows it, he keeps to himself. It is considered bad form among aboriginal tribes, I am told, to ask anyone's name, and it is seldom divulged until a firm basis of friendship is established."

Theodora Kroeber wrote that "Ishi was photographed so frequently and so variously that he became expert on matters of lighting, posing, and exposure. . . . Photographs of him were bought or made to be treasured as mementos along with family pictures and camera records of a holiday or an excursion."

I hear his name now in the isolation of this picture. You must imagine our lonesome pleasures in the poses that pleased the curators in the natural light near the museum at the University of California. Their dead voices haunt the margins of our photographs. We were not the last dreamers, or the last memories of our tribes, but we were the last to land in a museum as the simulations of a vanishing race.

Ishi may have been undressed above the waist for the photograph here by Joseph Kossuth Dixon, or one of his assistants, in connection with the last Rodman Wanamaker Expedition of Citizenship to the North American Indian in 1913.

Dixon outfitted a private railroad car and traveled to tribal communities and museums around the country. Later that year he published this portrait of Ishi, and more than a hundred other photographs from his collection, in *The Vanishing Race*.

"The Wanamaker expeditions took place at a time when the sense of national guilt about what had been done to the Indians was rising," wrote Charles Reynolds, Jr., in *American Indian Portraits from the Wanamaker Expedition of 1913* (Brattleboro, Vt.: Stephen Greene, 1971). "The Indians were seen as noble savages whom the white man had turned into a vanishing race." Ishi and Bluff Creek Tom are the only two "noble savages" who are not dressed to the neck in this collection of photographs.

Ishi posed for this "given" photograph, one of the few with his chest bared. The apparent tattoo on his chest does not appear in other photographs of him published in Theodora Kroeber's *Ishi in Two Worlds*. The tattoo, an intentional retouch or accidental stain on the negative, has never been explained.

Saxton Pope, the medical doctor who studied tribal archery, took Ishi to Buffalo Bill's Wild West Show when it was in town. A warrior from the show approached them. He touched Ishi's hair, looked into his face, and said, " 'He is a very high grade Indian.' As we left, I asked Ishi what he thought of the Sioux. Ishi said, 'Him's a big cheap.' "

Ishi was a winsome survivor, not a religious leader or a warrior chief on the road to simulations and representations. His personal power was more elusive than the political poses of a tribal leader. He was never obligated to speak as the last hunter of his tribe; otherwise, he might not have been heard even in the museum. His stories were his survivance, and not an obligation to be a tribal leader. He had a natural smile, but he never learned how to shake hands.

Pierre Clastres wrote in *Society Against the State* (New York: Zone Books, 1991) that a tribal chief must "prove his command over words. Speech is an imperative obligation for the chief." The leader "must submit to the obligation to speak; the people he addresses, on the other hand, are obligated only to appear not to hear him."

Some tribal leaders were captured as proud warriors in photographs; they were heard and overheard too much, and their stories were lost at inaugurations and postmodern performances in wild west shows. The simulated leaders lost their eminence in the discourse of tribal power, "because the society itself, and not the chief, is the real locus of power."

Clastres overturns the rustic notions of tribal leaders with a new sense of political responsibilities in communities. "The chief's obligations to speak, that steady flow of empty speech that he *owes* the tribe, is his infinite debt, the guarantee that prevents the man of speech from becoming a man of power."

Ishi was never heard as a tribal leader. He bared his chest and posed for photographs, but he was never decorated as a warrior. His portrait was published with a collection of other simulated tribal people. He posed for friends and photographers but was never invited to bare his chest in a wild west show.

"En route to the inauguration of President Wilson in 1913, thirty-two chiefs stopped in Philadelphia for the day to be entertained at the Wanamaker Store," wrote John Wanamaker in his contribution to *American Indian Portraits*. The special luncheon of warriors was followed by a "war dance" in a private corporate office.

Ishi lived in a museum and was not invited to the presidential inauguration. He was not a chief, but as a tribal survivor he could have been seen and heard as a leader. In a sense, he had more power than those who were invited to the inauguration as decorated warriors. Tribal power is more communal than personal, and the power of the spoken word goes with the survivors.

Ishi was at "ease with his friends," wrote Theodora Kroeber. He "loved to joke, to be teased amiably and to tease in return. And he loved to talk. In telling a story, if it were long or involved or of considerable affect, he would perspire with the effort, his voice rising toward a falsetto of excitement." His stories must have come from visual memories, and he should be honored because he never learned how to slow his stories down to be written.

"The Rodman Wanamaker Expedition of Citizenship to the North American Indian concluded in December 1913 with a ceremony on the Staten Island site where ground had been broken for the Indian memorial ten months earlier," wrote Charles Fergus in *Shadow Catcher* (New York: Soho Press, 1991), a novel based on the unusual photographic expedition.

"At the Panama-Pacific Exposition of 1915, in San Francisco, former president Theodore Roosevelt opened the exhibit of expeditionary photographs, and Joseph Dixon lectured three times a day for five months to more than a million citizens. Prints were sold from the three Wanamaker expeditions, perhaps the first photographic print sales on record," wrote Fergus in the novel's epilogue. "Dixon's illustrated book, *The Vanishing Race*, was also selling briskly; it has been reprinted several times over the years, with critics favorably comparing his photographs to the famous Indian portraits of Edward S. Curtis."

The Wanamaker photographs were forgotten in a few years' time; the collection landed in an attic and later in museums and archives. Those behind the cameras have vanished, but the last wild man and other tribal people captured in photographs have been resurrected in a nation eager to create a tragic past.

The Indian agent James McLaughlin, wrote Fergus, "was instrumental in persuading Franklin Lane, Secretary of the Interior under President Wilson, to speed the granting of citizenship to qualified Indians." The tribes were discovered, captured, removed to reservations, and photographed as outsiders in their own land. Ishi died eight years before he might have become a citizen of the mountains he told in stories. "McLaughlin designed tokens of citizenship that were presented in 1916 and 1917. These consisted of a purse . . . a leather bag, a button."

Ishi and then his picture ended in a museum. The photographers were lost on the margins; those who gazed at his bare chest and waited to shake his hand would vanish three generations later in a chemical civilization.

Ishi died at noon on March 25, 1916. Four days later the *San Mateo Labor Index* reported that the "body of Ishi, last of the Yano [Yahi] tribe of Indians, was cremated Monday at Mount Olivet cemetery. It was according to the custom of his tribe and there was no ceremony."

Jo Mora, *Hopi Kachina,* c. 1904. (Courtesy Jo Mora Collection, Cline Library, Special Collections and Archives, Northern Arizona University, Flagstaff.)

Jo Mora, *Hopi Dancers,* c. 1904. (Courtesy Jo Mora Collection, Cline Library, Special Collections and Archives, Northern Arizona University, Flagstaff.)

Ramona Sakiestewa

WEAVING FOR DANCE

I first saw these two photographs by Joseph Mora (1876–1947) in a 1979 exhibition catalogue from the Smithsonian (*The Year of the Hopi: Paintings and Photographs by Joseph Mora*). They were taken at the Snake Dance at Oraibi in 1904. They interested me, as a modern weaver, because they show what the dancers are wearing rather than what they are doing. In the first photograph, several figures are shown from the waist down. Their cotton kilts are embroidered with the traditional pattern, and some have sashes over the kilt in a cotton semi-brocade technique. The second photograph shows a kachina wearing a white manta embroidered on the bottom.

All of these fabrics evolved in the Southwest around A.D. 600, when cotton and weaving seem to have come from northern Mexico into the Four Corners area (southern Utah, southern Colorado, northern New Mexico, northern Arizona). They have varied in design since then, but the technique has remained the same. Cotton was grown up and down wet valleys like the Rio Grande Valley and Canyon de Chelly. It was already a dominant crop when the Spanish first made contact, and continued to be so until about 1900. Much of the cotton was grown in Arizona and then woven into fabric by Hopi and San Juan Pueblo and traded among other pueblos. A lot of cotton was also grown in northern New Mexico. The kilts in the Mora photographs are all hand-spun. They are not what we see today, which is commercially woven cotton cloth purchased and then embroidered.

Ceremonial clothing is made of five or six kinds of fabric: a plain black manta which becomes a dress; a large embroidered or plain cotton manta; embroidered kilts or plain painted kilts; and then two or three different sashes. There are over three hundred kachinas (or *katsinam*), the supernatural beings that represent not only individual life-forms, but Hopi cultural concepts. These basic fabrics are used in all their costumes. (Imagine your own daily wardrobe consisting of three skirts and two tops, or two pairs of pants and four shirts.) It was quite a feat to create over three hundred separate and distinct costumes, each reflecting the essence of a particular entity.

Almost every aspect of ceremonial activities has to do with bringing benevolent rain and fecundity to the community. The imagery on the kilt in the center of the first picture shows rain clouds and rain descending. The sashes are unique in their semi-brocade technique, which appeared after Spanish contact and does not exist anywhere else. They are woven in two panels and have alternate wool and cotton wefts running horizontally across the bottom. The two panels are woven separately and then sewn together in the middle. It has been speculated that these were influenced by the surplices of Catholic priests, although the imagery also resembles kachina masks. It is traditionally a red, green, and purple semi-brocade, and you see the pattern only on one side; on the reverse, it looks like a cotton ticking pattern. Today we see the same kind of sash, but semi-brocade sashes are now mostly embroidered. The newer ones are easily distinguishable because they are not nearly as fine as the earlier woven ones. When I first began living in Santa Fe, in 1966, there was a Hopi man who wove and sold these sashes. They cost about fifty dollars each. Today they are very difficult to find and are very expensive (about four hundred dollars).

The manta in the second photograph is approximately 54 × 64 inches; it has been folded in half so that you can see the back side of the embroidery; then it is brought around and pinned on one shoulder of the kachina to form the top. The lower garment is a black manta. The kachina also wears a white cotton finger-woven sash and under it, a striped shirt. This kachina is a Warrior Girl, called Kaletaka Mana, associated with the White Corn Girl groups, but all kachinas are men underneath. Mora did a very beautiful painting after this photograph. He wrote of it:

The White Hopi Butterfly ceremonial blanket was used, but the surface was reversed and instead of the well-done embroidery of the blanket it showed only the back of the stitches. This was odd enough, but what provoked me was that the dancer positively refused to take off the new striped brown shirt he was very proud of. When I cooled off, I went ahead and painted it just as I had seen it in the official dance, which, after all, was just as it should have been. Record only the authentic data even if it does not meet the artistic desire of the painter.[1]

I have never seen the manta reversed except for this kachina, although I have seen mantas that were doubled (two of them) or doubled over (the right side folded over). It is admirable that Mora recognized his own desire to make a perfect, conventional image and still submitted to the dancer's right to wear his new brown-striped shirt. This shows the level of Mora's human involvement with these people and further clarifies for me his genuine relationship to Hopis as individuals rather than as inanimate objects or subject matter.

Non-weavers see these photographs in terms of the overall aesthetic, but for me it is the tiny pieces of technical information that make them so wonderful. They help me understand a lot of subtle nuances in the weaving, the technique, and the application of how particular styles were wrapped or worn. For instance, another painting Mora did after a photograph shows a kachina wearing a red, white, and blue shawl. The fabric has curled edges along the vertical sides and one side has more of a pattern than the other. This was exciting for me to see because I had woven this same kind of twill-patterned "maiden shawl." As I wove, I realized that one side felt better than the other for some peculiar reason. So you come up with a piece that has a right and a wrong side. If you pull the yarn too tightly, your edges do curl substantially.

Joseph Jacinta Mora was born in Montevideo, Uruguay, on October 22, 1876. When he was not quite a year old, his parents (probably wealthy enough to be comfortable with two artist sons) emigrated to Boston, Massachusetts, where he later studied at Cowels Art School. Then he attended the Art Students League in New York City, returned to Boston to work, and in 1903 moved to San Jose, California, for reasons that are unclear. (According to my cousin Bob Ames, who lives in Salinas, Mora's relatives still live in that area.)

Also in 1903, Mora proposed to his Boston friend Walter Williams that they take a trip across California, over the Sierra Nevada mountains in the Mojave Desert into Arizona, specifically to see the Hopi Snake Dance. With two mules and a wagon, they made the trek, and Mora took many photographs of this amazing adventure through dust storms, rain, and snow. He remained in Arizona from 1904 to 1906, documenting and living at Hopi.

Mora's perceptions of the community in which he was a guest were vastly different from those of other photographers or anthropologists who have documented extensively at Hopi, such as H. C. Voth or Adam Clark Vroman. Mora's artistic sensibilities and his own personal philosophy somehow allowed him to see the community with different eyes. Instead of asking what the symbols meant, he saw the costumes themselves, their nuances, how they were assembled and made. He was not really mediating what he saw, but became a medium through which the community could be seen.

For me, however, these photographs are important because they document the end of a golden era of textiles and ceremonial costuming. Dry goods and store-bought materials became prevalent once the railroad reached into the West, and trade in woven goods among Indians waned. Today we have very few people with the technical knowledge and ability to weave what is now ceremonial costume but was once everyday wear. Mora documented the craft, the technique, the design, and the overall aesthetic.

There are a great number of photographs in the Mora Collection, now held at Northern Arizona University in Flagstaff. I feel more comfortable looking at his photographs than those of other photographers from the turn of the century because they more closely reflect what I see or have seen myself. Mora's is a tremendous legacy to the Hopi people.

Note:

1. Jo Mora, quoted in *Year of the Hopi: Paintings and Photographs by Jo Mora, 1904–1906* (New York: Rizzoli/Smithsonian Traveling Exhibition Service, 1979), p. 55.

Battleford Industrial School Football Team, Saskatchewan, 1897. (Courtesy Glenbow Museum, Calgary, Alberta, Canada.)

Gerald McMaster

COLONIAL ALCHEMY:

Reading the Boarding School Experience

*Of all the education the Indian people have received
they have never been told anything about their rights.
All of us who went to school over the years, not one
ever told us where we stood.*

—Cree Elder, John Tootoosis[1]

*By avoiding a detailed, contextual portrayal of Indian
culture on the prairies and by showing it in the distance,
Euro-Canadian discourse served and underlined its own
commitment to expansion of its empire. In so doing, it
dehumanized, trivialized and devalued the native way
of life.*

—Walter Hildebrandt[2]

Does knowledge of history build a stronger identity? Can photographs answer the elusive questions of a history that has been repeatedly suppressed?

My genealogical search began quite by accident in the archives of the Glenbow Museum in Calgary, Alberta, which houses the finest collection of photographs of the aboriginal peoples of the Canadian Plains. For years, partly out of blind faith, I believed that the "Edward Curtis" type of photograph—portraying the classic, majestic beauty of the Native North American—was the truth. But as I examined more photo collections, I realized that I was looking at a tragic history of my own ancestry. The complexity of our representation often equals the agony of distance many Native people experience when we see sacred and sensitive objects locked up in museum vaults or brutally displayed to the public.

As I became more interested in the countless photographs, I repeatedly wondered what they could prove. Do other Native people respond as I do? Could Native people scrutinize photograph collections and find a "historicity," a "true America" somewhere beneath all the exotica, erotica, simulacra? If so, what then is the potential, or latitude, for Native perspectives on history in the face of the prevailing disregard with which revisionist histories are greeted, even when they are written by white people?

Since much written about us by non-natives in the fields of art, anthropology, and literature is already viewed with skepticism by the Native communities, I am confident that Native artists and scholars can find appreciative Native audiences. As the crisis of representation reaches critical stages, an endorsement of new "Native perspectives" may be just around the corner. After all, each year brings new discourses on identity and on the tremendous impact of the colonial experience.

It was this colonial experience that stimulated my interest in the photograph of *Battleford Industrial School Football Team, 1897*. I had already seen many such images of Native people, but this one seemed different. First, I was surprised to discover that the "IS" stood for the Indian Industrial School at Battleford, Saskatchewan, the small town where I grew up. Then I discovered that the catalogue card listed all the boys' names. Too many photographs simply objectify "nameless" Native people. These boys not only had identities, but their names were familiar to me: Pooyak, Benson, Bear, Dakota, and Wuttunee. Their descendants survive on many of the reserves in the Battleford area. My own grandmother—Marie Isabella (Bella) Schmidt—attended the Industrial School from the age of six to sixteen (1904–1914).[3] After she left, she met and married George Wuttunee, sixteen years her senior. Two of his brothers appear in this photograph. The photographer, I thought, was sensitive enough to allow the boys the dignity of names. Recently I spotted this picture in a publication; this time, however, the boys were nameless, which made me all the more determined to give them back their identities.

> To be, or not to be—that is the question:
> Whether 'tis nobler in the mind to suffer
> The slings and arrows of outrageous fortune,
> Or to take arms against a sea of troubles,
> And by opposing, end them. . . .
> —William Shakespeare

Hamlet's famous soliloquy characterizes the question of identity and its retention in a crisis. In the football team photograph, I was amused by the rapid-fire repetition of the letters IS, IS, IS, IS, IS, which appear not as acronyms but as statements of being, as in Shakespeare's ultimate question. Punctuated by the medals as exclamation marks, the verb constitutes a claim to identity. Hidden within this photograph, I sense a crisis moments before the blink of the camera's shutter. These boys represent the first generation of Native children taken from their homes and forced into the alien environment of the white man's schools. Unlike many romantic photographs taken of Native people during the late nineteenth century (the period of "transition," when Native people were forced to give up their nomadic lives for the sedentary existence of the Indian Reserve), this image testifies to the tragedies Native people have endured in the last century.

Yet from my privileged position as observer (read: voyeur), these boys appeared defiant. I was intrigued by their apparent ambivalence about being photographed, indicated by clenched fist or folded arms. Despite their cropped hair and foreign clothes, an element of individuality persists. Even in the enforced, dehumanizing atmosphere of the Industrial School, these boys stand firm. Their trophies and medals suggest a group identity only in the European sense. Teamwork, from a Native perspective, was never so superficial. Since those early days of cultural intolerance, succeeding generations have resisted assimilation only at tremendous cost. This was what I sensed was wrong in the photograph. These boys represented the colonial experiment, a type of colonial alchemy: transforming the savage into a civilized human being. Yet somehow their resistance remains visible.

The Colonial Process
By the third quarter of the nineteenth century, most of the buffalo herds had been annihilated by hunters contributing to a Euro-Canadian/American economy. The loss of the buffalo was, of course, an economic and cultural disaster for all the Plains people. To the government, however, nomadism was unacceptable. It was too much trouble to have to keep a watchful eye on tribes while new settlers poured onto the Plains. Freely roaming Indians would impede the colonization process. "Reserve(d)" areas were thus conceived to coerce Native people into becoming sedentary farmers. It had taken centuries for Europeans to develop in this direction, but Native peoples were expected to change overnight.

The Canadian government's strategy was to convince tribal elders that there was no alternative to this process. In 1880 a new federal department was created under the Ministry of the Interior to oversee the affairs of Native people. Its mandate was simply to carry out a policy of assimilation, one stage of which was to educate all Native children. In 1874, the first Canadian Prime Minister, Sir John A. Macdonald, introduced the Indian Act, explaining that children had to be taken away from their parents in order to erase their savage influences, and to expose them to the benefits of Western civilization. The program was patterned after the U.S. framework policy of 1865. By 1884, Canada introduced the more lethal Indian Advancement Act, which called for the forced removal of young children from their homes.

Adults fared no better, as all their ancient customs and rituals were outlawed by the Indian Act.[4] It stated, for example, that "Every Indian or other person who engages in celebrating the Indian festival known as the 'Potlatch' or the Indian dance known as 'Tasmanawas' is guilty of a misdemeanor, and shall be liable to imprisonment for a term not more than six nor less than two months." Although the Potlatch was specific to the Northwest Coast, the law seemed to proscribe any Native religious manifestation, and led to a total devaluation of traditional cultures. Government officials had been lobbied by missionaries who were having difficulty winning converts. The campaign was ruthless, as further amendments to the Indian Act, in 1886 and 1887, enforced compulsory school attendance and ensured family separation.[5] Duncan Campbell Scott, Superintendent of Indian Affairs during the early part of the twentieth century, "believed that historical processes necessitated the death of the old order and that Indian culture was among those archaic forms."[6] "The Europeanization of the Indians" was simply part of the story of "progress."

For the next one hundred years, boarding schools dotted the Canadian landscape, leaving in their wake a legacy that has scarred many Native people. Forced removal broke up homes and families. Devastated mothers, fathers, and grandparents felt like prisoners on their own land. Legislators, however, insisted it was for the Indians' own good. Times were changing; the Indian now lived within the system of the white man. Yet not one aboriginal Canadian has ever signed the "social contract" to which all immigrants to Canada must agree—the social contract which is supposed to "melt" everyone into a Canadian citizen, culturally, sociopolitically, and economically. Thus the "distinctness" of aboriginal North Americans remains unchallenged and unparalleled. (In Canada we are called "First Nations" as opposed to the English, French, or Spanish "Founding Nations.") Native peoples will continue to protect that distinction "for as long as the grass grows and the sun shines . . ."

The Battleford Industrial School

The Industrial School was located in the building that served as the seat of government for the North West Territory from 1878 to 1883, when the capital moved south to Regina. Government House, as it was called, was then renovated as an Industrial School. It opened on December 10, 1883, with twelve students. Like most residential schools, it was situated not only far from the reserves but also far from white settlements. This helped lessen contact between children and their parents. The only adults present were those who ran the schools, and they were all non-Native. The schools were highly regimented and insisted on strict conformity. The military arrangements took away all forms of free expression usually available in tribal societies; but then, freedom of cultural and religious expression had already been denied by federal law. It was up to schools like Battleford to reinforce such laws, thus removing all traces of tribal and personal identity.

From the very beginning, the Indian Act legally arranged for provincial governments and religious organizations to provide Native education. Having the schools run by churches was cost-effective. The Roman Catholic, Anglican, United, and Presbyterian churches educated Native children in the ways of the white man. Even today, the Roman Catholic and Anglican churches continue to have an enormous impact.

According to the biographers of Cree Elder John Tootoosis, of Poundmaker Reserve, who attended the (Catholic) Delmas Residential School,

The missionaries heartily approved of [the] chance to convert and "civilize" the impressionable children, especially since the work was going slowly with the increasingly wary and resentful adults. . . . [The native people] were asking that they be taught to read and write, to learn with figures, to be trained into useful skills to enable them to compete on an equal basis. . . . The government violated deeply the spirit and intent of this most important (to the Indians) promise [to build and staff state schools]. The "education" provided was immediately subordinated to the conversion process and religious indoctrination.[7]

As the law commanded, all school-age children were taken from their homes and dispersed to various boarding schools throughout the Territory. When they arrived at the Industrial School, for instance, they were provided with plain, sufficient meals and clothing. They were given separate beds in dormitories, where they no doubt felt like birds in a tree—far from the earth in those high beds. This impersonal sleeping arrangement caused much loneliness and longing for home and family.

One of the first steps in the assimilation process was to impose new identities on the children. Cree Elder James Buller (Kasawapamat, or "He Who Looks Out") was seven years old in 1896 when he entered the first grade. He recalled:

The teachers couldn't pronounce our Indian names so they gave us new ones. They . . . gave everyone a last name. When it came to me they gave me the name of Buller. . . . The teachers also gave us first names too. Because I had [an English] first name already, they let me keep it. They named most boys after kings of England and most girls after queens. There were a lot of new students and too many were called the same first name. The teachers gave us middle names from the bible. Mine was Solomon.[8]

Boys received instruction in blacksmithing, carpentry, calcimining, painting, printing, shoemaking, farming, and gardening; girls learned baking, cooking, washing, mending, and other kinds of general housework. Other new customs included playing cricket against neighboring towns, performing music at local exhibitions, and organizing a brass band. The idea was for them to return to the reserves and pass on what they had learned. But in John Tootoosis's view, "Schools were oriented, not to prepare the children for their future role in life, but instead, to divorce them from their past."[9]

School rules prohibited the visiting of friends except at stated intervals. Buller recalled, "Boys and girls were not allowed to play together. The girls had their own play area. We never went near them at all. . . . I believe if you had a sister, there was a room where you were allowed to go and talk to her." School officials forbade students to speak in anything but English. Again, Buller: "We weren't allowed to speak Cree, none at all. But of course we spoke Cree after bedtime. I don't know if anyone got a licking if they were caught, but we were reprimanded alright; very seriously sometimes." As late as 1973, I visited an Indian school in northern Saskatchewan where a non-Indian teacher told us that she did not allow her students to talk on the telephone in anything but English. Old habits die hard.

The parents and grandparents must have been shocked when the children came home, for in their eyes the students would no longer be fit for the traditional way of life. John Tootoosis says:

The years of relentless brainwashing had served their purposes; the children had been almost totally alienated from their own background. . . . Having lost their Cree language, they could rarely understand what was being said, and could not make themselves understood, and it was months before it began to come back to them. They were strangers in their former homes. Their parents and grandparents, once the center of their existence, were now diminished, mere remnants of a bygone era and a worthless culture. They no longer could respect their Elders after having been so indoctrinated into the white man's religion. Cree songs and stories, ceremonies or prayers were now to these young converts terrifying evidence of souls damned and lost.[10]

The old warriors, hunters, chiefs, and elders could not predict the future, but they were losing the children who were their only source of hope as the death knell sounded for a once proud way of life.

In 1885, the Riel Rebellion, or Native Resistance, took place on the prairies. Many of the Cree and Blackfoot chiefs in the area supported the military resistance of the Métis against the establishment of British colonial rule. That year the stables at the Industrial School were burned, presumably by some local Native people, perhaps a sign of support for the resistance. The school was immediately closed. Buller recalls that every one of the students "escaped" from the school at that time. The Industrial School was forfeited to government troops under martial order, and was named Camp Otter. When the rebellion subsided that fall, the Reverend Clark returned to enlarge the school in order to house sixty new students along with a full staff of teachers and officers.

In later years, the school inherited a printing press from a publishing house in Winnipeg. Before long the students began to produce a semi-monthly newspaper called *The Guide*. When the Industrial School transferred out of direct government control and was taken over by the Church of England in 1895, it reported: "This is the oldest school of its kind in the Territories, having been established in 1883, twelve years ago. During that period, 186 students have been admitted—122 boys and 64 girls, and these have been taken from more than a dozen reserves scattered over a stretch of country about 250 miles long, from east to west."[11]

The Battleford Industrial School closed its doors in 1916, after thirty-three years. Students returned home to their respective reserves.[12]

The Football Team

Knowing the circumstances under which these boys were forcibly removed from their families, I wanted to know more about their defiance as the photographer "captured" their essences. There are so many contradictions in the picture. The boys were proud in their bearing as winners of a game; yet in a larger sense they were losers. The trophies, medals, and clothing suggest a colonial alchemy in process. Against this stands an aura of defiance, a personal and tribal identity maintained in the face of forced assimilation and acculturation. The boys make an effort to oppose the pressure of change, yet their cropped hair and new clothing signal a convincing retreat of identity. There is no individuality. They are reduced to lookalikes, in a military strategy to eliminate identity and personality.

Sports—football, soccer, or just plain horsing around—did much to take minds off routine chores. James Buller recalled, "We played a lot of sports. Different kinds of running and football, but soccer was our main game. We played against the [North West] Mounted Police and we played against the town." In pre–Industrial School days, these young boys would probably have been involved in other physical and competitive games, but without the missionaries looking on. How quickly, at the schools, they must have adjusted to the positions of "us" against "them."

Briefly then, who were these footballers?

· *Louis Laurent* was probably Métis, but little else is known.

· *Albert Peters* became a schoolteacher and later taught at Lesser Slave Lake.

- *Robert Bear.* Nothing is known of him, even though the name Bear, or Musqua, is well-known on several reservations.
- *Francis Bear.* Nothing known.
- *Baptiste Pooyak* was an Assiniboine born at Mosquito Grizzly Bear's Head Reserve. He later lived at Sweetgrass Reserve, west of Battleford. Pooyak is not the original native name, and was probably adopted at the school.
- *Joe Benson.* Nothing known, except that he was unrelated to the Bensons of Red Pheasant. The name Benson was known to be given freely to other students.
- *Gilbert Bear.* Nothing known.
- *Benjamin Dakota's* mother, Mary, was a Wuttunee, which made him a nephew to Peter and James Wuttunee, pictured with him. He is believed to have become a well-known long-distance runner, later joining the Edmonton Police Force. The name Dakota was later changed to Decoteau.
- *Robert Thomas* came from Le Pas, Manitoba.
- *James Wuttunee* was from Red Pheasant Reserve. He became a blacksmith, school-teacher, and organ player for the church.[13]
- *Peter Wuttunee* was James's half-brother, the youngest of the Wuttunee children. He was twelve years old at the time. Later he became a carpenter and, with James, did missionary work among the Native people.

The Wuttunees

As I said at the beginning, several of these boys' family names were familiar to me. The two Wuttunee boys grabbed my attention because that was my mother's maiden name. *Wuttunee*, which means "Eagle Tail Feathers," is a well-known name on the Red Pheasant Reserve, located eighteen miles south of the town of Battleford. Founded in 1878, it takes its name from Red Pheasant, who was the signatory for the band at the signing of Treaty No. 6, in 1876, when 121,000 square miles were ceded to the crown. Red Pheasant had two brothers: Wuttunee and Baptiste. Wuttunee, who was the actual Band Chief, did not agree to the provisions of the treaty and thus withdrew in deference to Red Pheasant; in so doing he relinquished his position. He died on July 21, 1904, outliving Red Pheasant by almost twenty years. The band was without a chief until the late 1930s, when George, one of Wuttunee's sons (and my grandfather), eventually received the title of hereditary chief.

The family names Wuttunee and Baptiste have survived. Chief Wuttunee had two wives—Maude and Marie (Manee)—and sixteen children. Under pressure to conform to Christian values, Wuttunee was painfully forced to "legally" marry Maude and to disavow Marie. George, who was born in 1882, married Marie Isabella Schmidt and my mother Lena was one of their seven children. George attended the day school on the reserve through grade two, and was not sent to the Industrial School. His brother Peter and half-brother James, who are in the photograph (first row, far right and second from right), had the misfortune of being born following the Indian Act legislation and so were required to attend the Industrial School.[14]

Many Native people believe that the cultural, religious and societal genocide was not to be blamed solely on the churches. The government used the churches to realize its assimilationist policies. Nonetheless, the participation of the churches in European imperialism has contributed immensely to alcoholism, family breakdown, and numerous other problems that torment Native communities across Canada and the United States. Today the boarding school is all but nonexistent in its original form—that is, administered by religious denominations for the sole purpose of conversion and assimilation. Many of Canada's original boarding school buildings still exist, some still operating as schools, albeit usually Indian-controlled, while others, like the old Battleford Industrial School, were destined to be torn down or transformed into museums. With so many repulsive stories about boarding school experience emerging from Native communities all across Canada and the United States, it would be more appropriate to turn them into historical sites, comparable to Alcatraz and Auschwitz, as reminders of the legalized atrocities of man against man.

One step in that direction is the recent and official apology of the Roman Catholic Oblate order for its role in the early education of Indian children at Canada's infamous Native residential schools, in the assimilation process that devastated Native culture, religion, and society. The Oblate Conference of Canada apologized for its role in the "mental, physical, and sexual abuse suffered by native youths who were forced by law to attend the schools." Its president, Reverend Doug Crosby, called the abuses "inexcusable, intolerable, and a betrayal of trust in one of its most serious forms."[15]

Colonial alchemy, in the form of compulsory school attendance and learning in this country's "two official languages," continues unabated here. Yet there are many Native communities who have taken control of their school systems. Now it is the Native people (ourselves) who must know past histories and recognize the fragile choices we make for our children's futures.

Notes:

1. John Tootoosis quoted in Jean Goodwill and Norman Sluman, *John Tootoosis* (Winnipeg: Pemmican Publications, 1984), p. 108.

2. Walter Hildebrandt, "Aesthetics and History: Image Makers and Aboriginal People," *Newest Review*, v. 16, no. 4, (April/May, 1991), p. 11.

3. Isabella was the only one of fourteen children to survive, and her mother, Mathilda Schmidt (*née* Lemire), a Roman Catholic Métis living in Battleford, vowed that if any of her children lived, she would have them attend the Anglican-run Industrial School. While Bella was a student, the Prime Minister, Sir Wilfrid Laurier, came to visit the school and she presented him with a bouquet; he shook her hand and kissed her on the cheek.

4. Douglas Cole and Ira Chaikin, in *An Iron Hand upon the People: The Law Against the Potlatch on the Northwest Coast* (Vancouver: Douglas and McIntyre, 1990) compare the ways this law affected Indian peoples of the west coast and those on the prairies: "[The prairie] experience was an almost exact duplication of that of the coastal natives. Ceremonial life was interrupted by the legislation, but forms of the ritual complex persisted widely. Surprisingly, there were many more arrests and imprisonments on the prairies for dancing and giving-away than in British Columbia" (pp. 175–76).

5. Sociologist James S. Frideres, in *Native People in Canada: Contemporary Conflicts* (Englewood Cliffs: Prentice Hall, 1983), states that the Indian Act, which was "originally designed both to protect the Native population and to ensure assimilation, has not weathered the centuries well. Not only has it structured inequality, poverty, and underachievement among Natives, but it has seriously encroached upon the personal freedom, morale, and well-being of Native people" (p. 32).

6. Cole and Chaikin, *Iron Hand*, p. 93.

7. Goodwill and Sluman, *John Tootoosis*, p. 27.

8. From unpublished transcripts of conversations with James Solomon Buller. I am especially indebted to his grandson, Ed Buller, for allowing me to use this material on his grandfather. Ed said it was gathered for the sake of his grandchildren so they will know their history, especially their family history.

9. Goodwill and Sluman, *John Tootoosis*, p. 95.

10. Goodwill and Sluman, *John Tootoosis*, p. 105.

11. Quoted in Vi Loscombe, "Government House Rendered Great Service," *North Battleford News Optimist*, circa 1895.

12. In Red Pheasant, another generation of schools had already opened: the Indian Day School. These schools were usually reserve-specific, providing education for band members. For those fortunate enough to attend day school, there was little regret for the boarding schools, because the students were free of many of the anxieties that came with displacement. They were no longer forced into "extracurricular" activities—pray, make beds, pray, do chores, and pray some more. In the day school there was freedom to play, visit, and speak in one's traditional language. Day schools were also considerably smaller and, at least in Red Pheasant, they were disassociated from religious denominations and run by government-appointed teachers.

By 1963–64, about 55,000 Native students were enrolled in elementary and secondary schools across Canada. Of these, 59 percent were in federal day schools, 13 percent were in residential schools, and 1 percent were in hospital schools. The remaining 27 percent attended integrated joint schools. The Red Pheasant Day School closed in 1962, and its twenty-five to thirty students went on to joint schools.

13. One of James Wuttunee's sons, William, later became a celebrated lawyer and author of *Ruffled Feathers: Indians in Canadian Society* (Calgary: Bell Books, 1971).

14. These names and brief historical accounts were gathered for me by my mother, Mrs. Lena McMaster, who conducted interviews with Harry Brabant, a respected traditional historian and Red Pheasant Cree Elder. Mr. Brabant is currently ninety-eight years old and was a student at the Battleford Industrial School beginning in 1907 when he was fourteen years old.

I also owe gratitude for wonderful conversation to my uncle George Wuttunee, brother of Lena, whose generous assistance in sorting out these names gave me more information on my family history:

Wuttunee and Maude had eight children: Thomas (b. 1873); George ((b. 1882), who married Marie Isabella and fathered Douglas, Bertha, Lena (my mother), Cecil, Oliver, George Jr., and Mabel; Peter (b. 1885), who is shown in the photograph; Emma; Mary (b. 1858), Harry Brabant's mother, who married Pierre Dakota and after he died married a Pambrun (her son Benjamin is in the photograph); Martha, who never married but had two children, Sarah (Soonias) and Gilbert Wuttunee; and Jessie, who was known to have married a white man and moved to Edmonton, going by the name of Latta. Very little is known of that side.

Wuttunee and Marie also had eight children: Isaac (b. 1883); Walter; David; James, who is in the photograph; two other boys whose names are unknown; a daughter whose first name is unknown but married into the Pechawis family of the Mistawasis Reserve; and Maggie (Soonias), who was the grandmother of the famous Plains Cree painter Allan Sapp. He immortalized her in many of his paintings.

15. Susan Mate, "RC Order Apologizes to Natives," *Calgary Herald*, July 24, 1991.

Marsie Harjo and Family. (Courtesy Joy Harjo.)

Marsie Harjo and Katie Menawe Harjo. (Courtesy Joy Harjo.)

Joy Harjo

THE PLACE OF ORIGINS

for my cousin John Jacobs (1918–1991), who will always be with me

I felt as if I had prepared for the green corn ceremony my whole life. It's nothing
I can explain in print, and no explanation would fit in the English language. All I
can say is that it is central to the mythic construct of the Muscogee people (otherwise known as "Creek"), a time of resonant renewal, of forgiveness.

The drive to Tallahassee Grounds in northeastern Oklahoma, with my friends
Helen and Jim Burgess and Sue Williams, was filled with stories. Stories here are
thick as the insects singing. We were part of the ongoing story of the people.
Helen and I had made a promise to participate together in a ceremony that ensures
the survival of the people, a link in the epic story of grace. The trees and tall, reed-
like grasses resounded with singing.

There's nothing quite like it anywhere else I've been, and I've traveled widely.
The most similar landscape is in Miskito country in northeastern Nicaragua. I
thought I was home again as I walked with the Miskito people whose homeland
had suffered terrible destruction from both sides in the war. The singing insects
provided a matrix of complex harmonies, shifting the cells in the body that shape
imagination. I imagine a similar insect language in a place I've dreamed in West
Africa. In summer in Oklahoma it's as if insects shape the world by songs. Their
collective punctuation helps the growing corn remember the climb to the sun.

Our first stop was Holdenville, to visit one of my favorite older cousins, John
Jacobs, and his wife Carol. They would join us later at the grounds. We traded
gifts and stories, ate a perfectly fried meal at the Dairy Queen, one of the few restaurants open in a town hit hard by economic depression. I always enjoy visiting
and feasting with these, my favorite relatives, and I feel at home in their house, a
refuge surrounded by peacocks, dogs, and well-loved cats, guarded by giant be-
neficent spirits disguised as trees.

Across the road an oil well pumps relentlessly. When I was a child in Oklahoma, the monster insect bodies of the pumping wells terrified me. I would duck down in the car until we passed. Everyone thought it was funny. I was called high-strung and imaginative. I imagined the collapse of the world, as if the wells were giant insects without songs, pumping blood from the body of Earth. I wasn't far from the truth.

My cousin John, who was more like a beloved uncle, gave me two photographs he had culled for me from family albums. I had never before seen my great-grandparents on my father's side. As I held them in my hand, reverberations of memory astounded me.

I believe stories are encoded in the DNA spiral and call each cell into perfect position. Sound tempered with emotion and meaning propels the spiral beyond three dimensions. I recognized myself in this photograph. I saw my sister, my brothers, my son and daughter. My father lived once again at the wheel of a car, my father who favored Cadillacs and Lincolns—cars he was not always able to afford but sacrificed to own anyway because he was compelled by the luxury of well-made vehicles, the humming song of a finely constructed motor. He made sure his cars were greased and perfectly tuned. That was his favorite music.

I was shocked (but not surprised) to recognize something I must always have known—the images of my great-grandmother Katie Menawe, my great-grandfather Marsie Harjo, my grandmother Naomi, my aunts Lois and Mary, and my uncle Joe. They were always inside me, as if I were a soul catcher made of a blood-formed crystal. I had heard the names, the stories, and perhaps their truths had formed the images, had propelled me into the world. My grandchildren and great-grandchildren will also see a magnification of themselves in their grandparents. It's implicit in the way we continue, the same way as corn plants, the same way as stars or cascades of insects singing in the summer. The old mystery of division and multiplication will always lead us to the root.

I think of my Aunt Lois's admonishments about photographs. She said that they could steal your soul. I believe it's true, for an imprint remains behind forever, locked in paper and chemicals. Perhaps the family will always be touring somewhere close to the border, dressed in their Sunday best, acutely aware of the soul stealer that Marsie Harjo hired to photograph them, steadying his tripod on the side of the road. Who's to say they didn't want something left to mark time in that intimate space, a space where they could exist forever as a family, a world drenched in sepia?

Nothing would ever be the same again. But here the family is ever-present, as is the unnamed photographer through his visual arrangement. I wonder if he was surprised to see rich Indians.

The parents of both my great-grandparents made the terrible walk of the Muscogee Nation from Alabama to Indian Territory. They were settled on land bordered on the north by what is now Tulsa—the place my brothers, my sister, and I were born. The people were promised that if they made this move they would be left alone by the U.S. government, which claimed it needed the tribal homelands for expansion. But within a few years, white settlers were once again crowding Indian lands, and in 1887 the Dawes Act, better known as the Allotment Act, was made law. Private ownership was forced on the people. Land that supposedly belonged in perpetuity to the tribe was divided into plots, allotted to individuals. What was "left over" was opened for white settlement. But this did not satisfy the settlers, who proceeded, by new laws, other kinds of trickery, and raw force, to take over allotments belonging to the Muscogee and other tribes. The Dawes Act undermined one of the principles that had always kept the people together: that land was communal property which could not be owned.

On December 1, 1905, oil was struck in Glenpool, Oklahoma. This was one of the richest lakes of oil discovered in the state. At its height it produced forty million barrels annually. Marsie Harjo's allotted land was in Glenpool. He was soon a rich man, as were many other Indian people whose allotted land lay over lakes of oil. Land grabs intensified. Many tribal members were swindled out of their property, or simply killed for their money. It's a struggle that is still being played out in the late twentieth century.

Oil money explains the long elegant car Marsie Harjo poses in with his family. In the stories I've been told, he always loved Hudsons. The family was raised in luxury. My grandmother Naomi and my Aunt Lois both received B.F.A. degrees in art and were able to take expensive vacations at a time when many people in this country were suffering from economic deprivation. They also had an African-American maid, whose name was Susie. I've tried to find out more about her, but all I know is that she lived with the family for many years and made the best ice cream.

There are ironies here, because Marsie Harjo was also half or nearly half African-American, and in more recent years there has been racism directed at African-Americans by the tribe, which originally accepted Africans and often welcomed them as relatives. The acceptance of slavery came with the embrace of European-American cultural values. It was then that we also began to hate ourselves for our own darkness. It's all connected: ownership of land has everything to do with the ownership of humans and how they are treated, with the attitude toward all living things.

This picture of my great-grandparents' family explodes the myth of being Indian in this country for both non-Indian and Indian alike. I wonder how the image of a Muscogee family in a car only the wealthy could own would be interpreted by another Muscogee person, or by another tribal person, or by a non-Indian anywhere in this land. It challenges the popular culture's version of "Indian"—an image that fits no tribe or person. By presenting it here, I mean to question those accepted images that have limited us to cardboard cut-out figures, without blood or tears or laughter.

There were many photographs of this family. I recently sent my cousin Donna Jo Harjo a photograph of her father Joe as a child about five. He was dressed in a finely tailored suit and drove a child's-size model of a car. His daughter has never lived in this kind of elegance. She lives on her salary as a sorter for a conglomerate nut and dried fruit company in northern California. She loves animals, especially horses and cats. (Our clan is the Tiger Clan.) I wonder at the proliferation of photographs and the family's diminishment in numbers to this present generation.

The second photograph is a straight-on shot of the same great-grandparents standing with two Seminole men in traditional dress, wearing turbans. They are in stark contrast to my great-grandparents—especially Marsie Harjo, who is stately and somewhat stiff with the fear of God in his elegant white man's clothes, his Homburg hat.

Marsie Harjo was a preacher, a Creek Baptist minister, representing a counterforce to traditional Muscogee culture. He embodied one side in the split in our tribe since Christianity was introduced and the people were influenced by European cultural values; the dividing lines remain the same centuries later. He was quite an advanced thinker, and I imagine he repressed what he foresaw for the Muscogee people, who probably would not have believed him anyway.

My great-grandfather was in Stuart, Florida, as he was every winter, to "save" the souls of the Seminole people. He bought a plantation there, and because he hated pineapples, he had every one of the plants dug up and destroyed. I've also heard that he owned an alligator farm. I went to Stuart this spring on my way to Miami and could find no trace of the mission or the plantation anywhere in the suburban mix of concrete, glass, and advertisements. My memories are easier to reach in a dimension that is as alive and living as anything in the three dimensions we know with our five senses.

My great-grandmother Katie Menawe is much more visible here than in the first photograph, where she is not up front, next to the driver, but in the very back of the car, behind her four children. Yet she quietly presides over everything as she guards her soul from the intrusive camera. I sense that Marsie boldly entered the twentieth century ahead of most people, while Katie reluctantly followed. I doubt if she ever resolved the split in her heart between her background and foreground.

I don't know much about her. She and her siblings were orphaned. Her sister Ella, a noted beauty, was my cousin John's mother. They were boarded for some time at Eufaula Indian School. I don't know how old Katie was when she married Marsie Harjo. But the name Monahwee* is one of those Muscogee names that is charged with memory of rebellion, with strength in the face of terrible adversity. Tecumseh came looking for Monahwee when he was building his great alliance of nations in the 1800s. Monahwee was one of the leaders of the Red Stick War, an armed struggle against the U.S. government to resist Andrew Jackson's demand for the removal of the tribes from their Southeastern homelands. Creeks, Seminoles, and Africans made up the fighting forces. Most of those who survived went to Florida, where the Seminoles successfully resisted colonization by hiding in the swamps. They beat the United States forces, who were aided by other tribes, including other Creeks who were promised land and homes for their help. The promises were like others from the U.S. government. Those who assisted were forced to walk west to Indian Territory like everyone else.

Monahwee stayed in Alabama and was soon forced west, but not before he joined with Jackson's forces to round up Seminoles for removal to Oklahoma. My cousin John said he died on the trail. I know that he died of a broken heart. I have a McKenney Hall portrait print of Monahwee, an original hand-colored lithograph dated 1848. Katie has the same eyes and composure of this man who was her father.

By going to Tallahassee Grounds to take part in a traditional tribal ceremony, I was taking my place in the circle of relatives, one more link in the concatenation of ancestors. Close behind me are my son and daughter, behind them, my granddaughter. Next to me, interlocking the pattern, are my cousins, my aunts and my uncles, my friends. We dance together in this place of knowing beyond the physical dimensions of space, much denser than the chemicals and paper of photographs. This place is larger than mere human memory, than the destruction we have walked through to come to this ground.

Time can never be stopped, rather it is poised so we can make a leap into knowing or into a field of questions. I understood this as we stompdanced in the middle of the night, as the stars whirred overhead in the same patterns as when Katie, Marsie, and the children lived beneath them. I heard time resume as the insects took up their singing again, to guide us through memory. The old Hudson heads to the east of the border of the photograph. For the Muscogee, East is the place of origins, the place the People emerged from so many hundreds of years ago. It is also a place of return.

*His name is sometimes spelled Menawe or Menewa, but on his gravestone in Okmulgee, Oklahoma, it is spelled Monahwee.

Robert Chaat (?), four glass slides, 1920s or early 1930s.
(Courtesy Paul Chaat Smith.)

Paul Chaat Smith

EVERY PICTURE TELLS A STORY

History records that Ishi, a.k.a. the Last Yahi, the Stone Age Ishi Between Two Worlds, was captured by northern Californians in 1911 and dutifully turned over to anthropologists. He spent the rest of his life in a museum in San Francisco. (And you think your life is boring.)

They said Ishi was the last North American Indian untouched by civilization. I don't know about that, but it's clear he was really country and seriously out of touch with recent developments. We're talking major hayseed here, at least.

His keepers turned down all vaudeville, circus, and theatrical offers for the living caveman, but they weren't above a little cheap amusement themselves. One day they took Ishi on a field trip to Golden Gate Park. An early aviator named Harry Fowler was attempting a cross-country flight. You can imagine the delicious anticipation of the anthropologists. The Ishi Man *vs.* the Flying Machine. What would he make of this miracle, this impossible vision, this technological triumph? The aeroplane roared off into the heavens and circled back over the park. The men of science turned to the Indian, expectantly. Would he quake? Tremble? Would they hear his death song?

Ishi looked up at the plane overhead. He spoke in a tone his biographers would describe as one of "mild interest." "White man up there?"

Twenty years later my grandfather would become the first Comanche frequent flyer. Robert Chaat was born at the turn of the century in Oklahoma, when it was still Indian Territory. It was our darkest hour. The Comanche Nation was in ruins, wrecked and defeated. The Army did a census at this time and found that 1,171 of us were still alive.

Grandpa Chaat was one of those holocaust survivors. He was a tireless fighter for the Jesus Road, who battled the influence of peyote and forbade his children to attend powwows. Yet he also taught pride in being Indian and conducted services in Comanche into the late 1960s. His generation was pretty much raised by the Army, who beat them for speaking Indian and had them march like soldiers to school. Geronimo was the local celebrity, and my grandfather remembers meeting him before the old guy died in 1909. Fort Sill was a small place; I guess everyone knew Geronimo.

My mother remembers her dad's trips to Chicago and New York when air travel was often a two-day adventure. He sent his five children trinkets from the 1939 World's Fair, newspaper clippings about his speeches around the country, pictures of himself with Norman Vincent Peale.

She discovered the lantern slides on a trip back to Oklahoma in 1991. They were in a battered and ancient black case buried deep in a closet. These closets have given up more and more secrets as time has passed. A few years earlier, when Grandpa still lived in the tiny house in Medicine Park (soon he would move to a nursing home in town) he produced an eagle feather from one of those closets. The feather, he told my mother, belonged to an ancestor who was a medicine man.

The forty-eight square glass slides are about three by four inches, at least an eighth of an inch thick. Each has its own slot in the felt-lined case. They're heavy: a single one weighs more than an entire box of their modern equivalents. Generously engineered with metal and glass instead of cardboard and film, they are about as similar to today's slides as a 1937 Packard is to this year's Honda.

They show Indian lodges, tipis, Comanches of all ages in brilliant clothing, buffalo, horses, wagons, Quanah Parker's Star House, all in vivid, lifelike color.

Their meaning and purpose? Fund-raising, of course. There were even a few pledge cards scattered about the case, reading: "Indian Mission Fund. I pledge to pay the sum of _____ before May 1, 19____." I could see Grandpa lugging his twenty pounds of glass slides through airports (still called "fields") because they would have been too precious to check through, the key to next year's budget or the church's building fund.

But what were these pictures? Mom could identify some of the locations and people, but most of them she could not. Maybe they weren't even Comanche. Perhaps the Dutch Reformed Church had a media consultant who put it together. The label points in this direction—it says: "Chas. Beseler Co., New York," not some outfit in Lawton or Oklahoma City. Grandpa might have sent along a few of his own pictures, and the rest, for all we know, might have been from a photo agency in Manhattan.

To me the Indians in the pictures seem dignified, friendly, open to religious instruction and new cultural ideas. I imagine listening to Grandpa in a church meeting room in New York or Boston in 1937, hearing about the struggle for redemption and a better way of life. A people at a crossroads, he might say. The images underline his script: Indians in blankets with papooses on their back next to Indians in starched western shirts and bandannas, posing for the camera on their way to a Jimmie Rodgers show. We see, ridiculously, an umbrella next to a wagon.

Which will it be, the blanket or the Bible?

On second thought, it's obvious the Indians are resistance fighters pretending to cooperate. See that look in their eyes? They are American hostages denouncing imperialism in a flat, dull voice for the Hezbollah. They steal the photographer's gun when he's not looking. At the gourd dance tonight in the foothills of Mount Scott, they make plans for the future, plans the city fathers won't like.

We have been using photography for our own ends as long as we've been flying, which is to say as long as there have been cameras and airplanes. The question isn't *whether* we love photography, but instead *why* we love it so much. From the Curtis stills to our own Kodachrome slides and Polaroid prints and Camcorder tapes, it's obvious we are a people who adore taking pictures and having pictures taken of us.

So it should hardly be a surprise that everything about being Indian has been shaped by the camera.

In this relationship we're portrayed as victims, dupes, losers, and dummies. Lo, the poor fool posing for Edward Curtis wearing the Cheyenne headdress even though he's Navajo. Lo, those pathetic Indian extras in a thousand bad westerns. Don't they have any pride?

I don't know, maybe they dug it. Maybe it was fun. Contrary to what most people (Indians and non-Indians alike) now believe, our true history is one of constant change, technological innovation, and intense curiosity about the world. How else do you explain our instantaneous adaptation to horses, rifles, flour, and knives?

The camera, however, was more than another tool we could adapt to our own ends. It helped make us what we are today.

See, we only became Indians once the armed struggle was over in 1890. Before then we were Shoshone or Mohawk or Crow. For centuries North America was a complicated, dangerous place full of shifting alliances between the United States and Indian nations, among the Indian nations themselves, and between the Indians and Canada, Mexico, and half of Europe.

This happy and confusing time ended forever that December morning a century ago at Wounded Knee. Once we no longer posed a military threat, we became Indians, all of us more or less identical in practical terms, even though until that moment, and for thousands of years before, we were as different from one another as Greeks are from Swedes. The Comanches, for example, were herded onto a reservation with the Kiowa and the Apache, who not only spoke different languages, but were usually enemies. (We hated Apaches even more than Mexicans.)

The truth is we didn't know a damn thing about being Indian. This information was missing from our Original Instructions. We had to figure it out as we went along.

The new century beckoned. Telegraphs, telephones, movies; the building blocks of mass culture were in place, or being invented. These devices would fundamentally change life on the planet. They were new to us, but they were almost as new to everyone else.

At this very moment, even as bullets and arrows were still flying, Sitting Bull joined Buffalo Bill's Wild West Show and became our first pop star. Like an early Warhol he sold his autograph for pocket change, and like Mick Jagger he noticed that fame made getting dates easier. He toured the world as if he owned it, made some money, became even more famous than he already was. Afraid of cameras? *Talk to my agent first* is more like it.

It was an interesting career move, even if it couldn't prevent the hysterical U.S. overreaction to the Ghost Dance that resulted in his assassination the same month as the Wounded Knee massacre.

Some think of Sitting Bull as foolish and vain. No doubt Crazy Horse felt this way. The legendary warrior hated cameras and never allowed himself to be photographed, although this didn't stop the U.S. Postal Service from issuing a Crazy Horse stamp in the 1980s. Maybe Sitting Bull was ego-tripping, but I see him as anxious to figure out the shape of this new world.

For John Ford, King Vidor, Raoul Walsh and the other early kings of Hollywood, the Indian wars were more or less current events. Cecil B. DeMille, who made over thirty Indian dramas, was fifteen at the time of Wounded Knee. They grew up in a world in which relatives and friends had been, or could have been, direct participants in the Indian wars.

The promise of film was to deliver what the stage could not, and the taming of the frontier, the winning of the West, the building of the nation was the obvious, perfect choice. Indians and Hollywood. We grew up together.

This has really screwed us sometimes, for example the stupid macho posturing by some of our movement leaders in the 1970s. (If only their parents had said, *Kids! Turn that TV off and do your homework!* we might have actually won our treaty rights.)

But maybe it's better to be vilified and romanticized than completely ignored. And battles over historical revisionism seem doomed from the start, because the last thing these images are about is what really happened in the past. They're fables being told to shape the future.

All of the lame bullshit, the mascots, the pickup truck commercials, the New Age know-nothings, I used to find it embarrassing. Now I think it's part of the myth to think all that is bogus and the good old days were the real thing. The tacky, dumb stuff about this country is the real thing now. The appropriation of Indian symbols that began with the earliest days of European contact is over, complete. Today, nothing is quite as American as the American Indian. We've become a patriotic symbol.

For our part, we dimly accept the role of Spiritual Masters and First Environmentalists as we switch cable channels and videotape our weddings and ceremonies. We take pride in westerns that make us look gorgeous (which we are!) and have good production values. We secretly wish we were more like the Indians in the movies.

And for the Americans, who drive Pontiacs and Cherokees and live in places with Indian names, like Manhattan and Chicago and Idaho, we remain a half-remembered presence, both comforting and dangerous, lurking just below the surface.

We are hopelessly fascinated with each other, locked in an endless embrace of love and hate and narcissism. Together we are condemned, forever to disappoint, never to forget even as we can't remember. Our snapshots and home movies create an American epic. It's fate, destiny. And why not? We are the country, and the country is us.

(What? No flash again?!)

Family Portrait, c. 1958. (Courtesy Suzanne Benally.)

Suzanne Benally

WOMEN WHO WALK ACROSS TIME

Tsiitchii' Bitsi
She greets
the rising sun
in the eastern horizons

This photograph was taken around 1958–59. Pictured are my great-grandfather Hastiin Tseyi Hocho' (Man Who Comes from Evil Canyon), my great-grandmother Tsiitchii' Bitsi (Redhair's Daughter), and my grandmother Ak'iniibaa' (Has Met Her Objective in War). I often look at this photograph as a way of understanding the complexity, and at times confusion, of my own life. The photo is not a still representation of any moment in time, but rather a glimpse of the continuing lives of my family in a pivotal period—those of my mothers (great-grandmother, grandmother, mother, aunts) and myself and my daughters. The photo is simply a part of our story, which we continue to shape, to live, which is to tell.

Red sandstone mesas rise and curve
around the horizon
extending like protective arms
to form a cove called Red Valley.
This is my home.

At about the time this photo was taken, I was a child playing around the hogan while a sheep that had just been butchered was being prepared inside. I loved to climb around on the red sandstone rocks, searching the pocketholes in the rocks' surfaces for small treasures. I played endlessly, dancing, skipping around the rocks, moving freely in and out of the adult busy-ness, as all children do. Occasionally I would glance toward the hogan and shadehouse, where the cooking was taking place, for assurance, made hungry by the smells coming from that direction. This day's activity was like any other day's, except that I still remember my four-year-old humility and embarrassment at being in the wrong place at the wrong time.

Tired of playing, I went to the hogan looking for my mother and as I arrived at the door I was shocked by a splash of water that covered me from head to toe. As I looked down I saw my new pair of white socks turning pink from the blood in the water. As I looked up I heard my great-grandmother crying out, "I threw the dirty water on the baby." I also heard the yells and laughter from my mother and aunts who scolded me for being in the way. My nearly blind great-grandmother had been cleaning the sheep and as usual tossed the rinsing water right out the door. I was embarrassed and angry and ran to hide till I had the courage to re-appear. The cooking and meal preparations continued as if nothing had happened and I learned humility as I deferred to my great-grandmother's blindness and natural ways.

In telling this story, I am struck and puzzled by the white socks I wore. In some ways they are significant in my memory of this event. It would have been unusual for me to be wearing a new pair of white socks. But as I look at the photograph, perhaps not. Standing behind my great-grandparents in the picture is my grand-mother as a young woman. Change is evident in her cut and curled hair, yet she remains in traditional clothing. My grandmother was one of the few children who left the tight extended family as a young woman and went to work for mission-aries. Up until that time, the story goes, my great-grandfather—mistrustful of the white man—had managed to keep the missionaries at bay with his rifle. He feared they would take his children.

My grandmother's leaving distinguished her and set her apart from the rest of the family. There are times when I'm walking down the street in a large city and I stop to look up at the high-rising buildings and try to comprehend how I got to what I am and what I am doing there. In many ways I am the continuance of my grandmother's departure through a couple of generations. My mother continued to move into the dominant white world through her education, and I further this by my college degrees, living and working in a city. The photograph reminds me of my roots, my home, my family, but my grandmother's cut hair also reminds me of my severance (by way of change) from that once tight extended family. The cut hair symbolizes loss, the beginning of a changed course.

My grandmother's leaving was to pave our way into an unknown future. Her break from the family was a break from a direct cultural and traditional life style. The consequence of my grandmother's choice was a journey of negotiating two worlds, that of the dominant American society and that of the Diné people. As I look at the course of my grandmother's life, and my mother's, I see the in and out, the moving back and forth that occurred. I see the way in which these women brought their cultural lives into a world of struggle, yet maintained the values and beliefs of being Navajo and drew strength from them.

My grandmother was a courageous woman. She walked into a world that never gave her peace and has given her descendents little peace. Perhaps she never understood why she walked away and into a foreign world. Or perhaps she recognized a need to confront a changing time. Perhaps she desired the white man's world. Perhaps in a moment, that thin sliver of time, she simply walked into the future in absence of thought.

I've never quite appreciated photographs and have rarely taken them, even of my children. I've felt that the life we live and the stories we hear and tell are the real and imaginative substance called memory. I'm not sure what it is photos truly capture, or how they speak to us as visual representations. We don't create them as we might a piece of art. We don't tell or write a story as a creation with photos, we don't dance nor do we sing with photos.

The elements that give and sustain life—wind, air, sound, water—don't move through photographs. Our spirits don't move through photos yet something is caught in that moment of time and space. Something of ourselves unrecognizable at that moment. Is this the moment of change?

I look at this photo and think of how the picture must have been arranged. I can't be sure that my great-grandparents really knew that their picture was being taken and what this meant to them if they did. I suspect that they were seated, a snapshot was taken, and they have never seen the results. How were they to make sense of a photograph, of a box that produced a still representation, the very image of themselves, but without color? How were they to make meaning of a small black box that stops for a moment the wind, air, light, sound—and holds that moment forever? Is this what old people feared when they believed their spirits were being captured? What was the person who took the photo (probably an aunt) trying to capture, to hold on to?

I move from this photo to another (not shown) that pictures my firstborn daughter held by her great-great-grandmother as her great-grandmother, grand-

103

mother, and I stand around. Looking at the five generations of women I realize the way my daughter has become part of the story (not merely an addition to the photo) and how through her life she will tell and retell the story. The photo captures the passing on of story as her great-great-grandmother sings memory into her. The photo has caught a glimpse of our lives at another pivotal moment of change. This time my great-grandmother has grown wiser and knows what has passed over time and gives to my daughter our lives to carry on. Perhaps we've only taken photographs at these pivotal moments, to make points of change and continuance.

Women who walk across time
appear in the horizon
coming to us with children in their arms.
Carrying forth
the winds, that blow spirits, the earth
into sky, moons passing,
sun's eastern warriors at dawn
as stars spin out of galaxies,
bringing that spark, spinning past onward
to unknown times
stars that remain fixed
guiding our children out of the past
to the future
stars that remain in ancient telling patterns.
As we become
the women who walk across time
appearing in the horizon
bringing with us children in our arms.

Jolene Rickard

CEW ETE HAW I TIH: THE BIRD THAT CARRIES LANGUAGE BACK TO ANOTHER

According to us, the Ska ru re (Tuscarora), it was a woman called Mature Flowers, or Mature Earth, who first tumbled through the sky world to this world. Her fall was broken by the united backs of waterfowl, and she was gently eased onto the back of a great turtle. On this tiny earth, she began at once to walk about, throwing dirt, causing it to grow. Mature Flowers, the first mother, brought with her the seeds of our life—corn, beans, squash, and tobacco—and so it continues . . .

Did all my grandmothers walk through time to be forgotten in their sleep? They send us reminders, tell us no. A quiet celebration of the initial planting of life is still stitched, woven, shaped, scraped, brushed, danced, and echoed in song into our memory. Our cultural clues expose both the net of colonization and the ongoing fight/celebration of resistance.

A familiar sight: three Indian women sitting in a booth selling what they have made. This particular bark-and-nail booth was on the grounds of "Indian Village" at the New York State Fair, near the territories of the Onondaga people. It's probably still there, but the women who once sat there are long gone, and new ones keep coming.

One such woman was my great-grandma, Florence Nellie Jones Chew, at the left of this photograph. The shadow of a beaded jitterbug has fallen on her cheek. The middle woman is my cousin, Louise Falling Husk Henry—Turtle Clanmother. The woman shadowed at the right is Mina Brayley. All three from Ska ru re.

The photograph of these three women was taken sometime during late summer in the 1940s, but before 1947, because that's when my great-grandma Flossie passed away. The collage was done in 1992. The first thought that came to my

Jolene Rickard, Photomontage, 1992. (Courtesy Jolene Rickard.)

mother's mind when I asked her about Grandma Flossie was her unconditional generosity. Mother remembers large bins of four or five different types of apples, pears, potatoes, beans, squash in her root cellar. Anybody who came to her home was offered as much as they wanted from the bins. Flossie would always say, "Go ahead, take as much as you need." Since her husband, Willy Chew, was chief of the White Bear Clan and held the enrollment book, people were always dropping by. My great-grandma clung to the belief that it was the duty of the chiefs of the Ska ru re Nation to share whatever they had, thereby setting an example of humility. The people to whom she offered felt comfortable enough to take what they could use. They probably needed it. Times were pretty tough on the reservation before, during, and after the Depression. There was no government relief and my people did not amass great monetary fortunes out of the oppression of other people and resources.

Truth was, the Ska ru re had been subjected to a process of cultural reconstruction since our migration from the land of the floating pine (North Carolina) in the mid-1700s. As early as 1585 the Ska ru re had sporadic contacts with the British, escalating to a full-blown war by 1711. A century of constant pressure from the British and their Indian allies finally forced us to migrate for our survival. The Ska ru re were formally adopted by the Iroquois as the Sixth Nation of the Confederacy by 1723. It was my great-grandma Flossie's grandmother who walked from North Carolina to where we live today, near the "thundering waters" of Niagara Falls. The Seneca people gave us a gift of one square mile and we worked and purchased the rest of our land.

Initially we survived as growers. The year after my great-grandma Flossie was born in 1891, the U.S. Census Office filed a report on Ska ru re. Its tone indicated obvious surprise at the productivity of our orchards, gardens, and grain fields. The shock at our ability to survive might well have been based on the knowledge of what we had been through. Such refusal to recognize indigenous peoples' ingenuity for survival is just another tactic in the colonizing process. By not recognizing our continuity as a separate and self-governing people, the U.S. government felt no need to observe their own laws and treaties.

A culturally mutual "sizing up" took place as early as the fur-trade days. The colonial gaze has never really ceased, and time has proven that it is never unintentionally directed. The darkest examples of this constant observation include the work of anthropologists, the policies of the Bureau of Indian Affairs, and the FBI's COINTELPRO activities against any Indian movement for human rights. Outwardly more innocent exchanges took place in the booths of the New York State Fair, Indian Markets, trading posts, and in Hollywood's promotions, from Tonto and the

Lone Ranger to Kevin Costner and *Dances with Wolves*. And in the ever-present photographer.

Remember, indigenous people come from an oral tradition. The written word has only had real impact in the past two centuries. The relationship between the oral tradition and the mnemonic objects that serve it—the wampum belt, the condolence cane, the sacred tobacco, the rattles—continues to this day. In my community there is a relationship between all the objects that we create and the words that surround us. The words are here to teach and guide us through life; the objects are here to serve the memory and meaning of the word. The practice of looking at things to remember is our way. In the past it served the truth. Whose "truth" do we observe when we look at photographs?

The bark booths at the New York State Fair have become for me a classic projection of Indian people's place in this economy. Everyone knows that Indian handicrafts are harmless. But what is really negotiated in this trade of money for what we create? The people from Ska ru re and most other Indian nations developed specific items for this exchange. The dangling "jitterbug" pins made from odd beads, like the elaborately beaded pillows, birds, and pin cushions, are really messengers. What we create, tourist item or not, serves as a reminder of our spiritual, economic, and cultural survival. The strongest remaining symbols amongst the Ska ru re are the beadwork and the white corn.

The beadwork embodies a continued visual connection to the "power of the good mind." When this world was created, the grandsons of Mature Flowers walked the earth and created all the things that would help us to live and to destroy life. Night and day, the four-legged and the winged, the medicines and berries, both helpful and harmful—all of these things are held in balance by "the power of the good mind," revered in the time spent putting millions of tiny drops of glass onto hides or fabric. Ska ru re beadwork not only brings the knowledge from the past to our young ones, but at a critical point in our adaptation to relocation, it actually put food in our mouths.

Beads have historically been a catalyst for trade. Shells, the first form of beads, demonstrated an extensive trade network between the Americas well before contact. In the post-contact period, the beads became glass and were much sought-after by my people. They shaped our trade relationship with the Europeans in ways that remind me of multinational corporations removing people from the land today, destroying their subsistence, stealing their resources, leaving them with no option but that of wage labor. Trading beads—like "trading" inappropriate technology and unwanted borders to "developing" governments—was part of this exploitation. Land rights were traded away for glass beads and other European material culture. "Trade" is the wrong word in this context. Force, coercion, manipulation describe more clearly what has happened.

But with these beads my grandmothers made souvenirs to sell and served our beliefs as well. This strategy must be acknowledged as part of the beadwork. Did they know the beads would carry not only physical representations of our understanding of all the living things on this earth, but also a message, a measure of time to adjust to the changes that whirl through our existence? It takes time to put thousands of tiny beads on cloth; it teaches you the patience to observe, the ability to see things as a whole or a multitude of parts. It is important to see how things are connected and what gives them life.

In the early 1800s, the American public's imagination was focused on the sublime qualities of the falling waters at Niagara. The Ska ru re sold many a beaded piece to tourists flocking to stand near this force of nature. We made the objects specifically for this trade and they have been identified by antique dealers as "whimsies." When I polled the beadworkers and others in my community, no one referred to the beadwork in this way. Who has the right to name this art? Only the Ska ru re.

These beaded pieces were closely linked to the visitors' experiences at the falls. By the mid-1800s, Niagara Falls was surrounded by tourist traps, hucksters, and amusements. An "Indian" souvenir was part of the trip. The beadwork meant economic and cultural survival for the Ska ru re. For the tourist, it was a connection to the mysterious force buried in the carnival atmosphere around the falls. Today a piece like the one represented in my photo-collage would be sold for around $125.

As I look at this image of my great-grandma Flossie and her friends in the Indian Village at the New York State Fair, I chuckle at those silly bark booths and marvel at her willingness to continue this kind of inevitably lopsided cultural exchange. The money put down on the table is merely a token. What is really being purchased is a momentary release from the crimes of the past.

My great-grandma was truly generous.

I, on the other hand, am less generous about how we are represented. I am less willing to let this photo stand as it is. Without an accompanying text, it suggests a passive acceptance of great-grandma's role as "Indian selling exotica to the curious." For this reason, I hesitated to use this photograph, to risk reinforcing another stereotype. Yet I wanted to deal with what Ska ru re create and why it is significant. So in the photo-collage, I changed the scale relationship between my great-grandma and the beadwork she created, to avoid the possibility of further misrepresentation and to focus the observer on the beadwork, which is much more important than generally thought.

Jitterbugs are the little dangling stick figures at the top of the booth. They are made from odd buttons, scrapped jewelry, mixed beads, and wire. The little twisted figures sold for twenty-five cents in the past and were made mainly by young fingers. They were where you started to learn about beadwork. They had little safety pins on their tops. As children, we wore them around for decoration, sometimes five or ten at a time. Those wiry little bodies had personality. In my imagination they weren't children, but jitterbug people.

The bird, flowers, and cherries to feed the birds were a common theme for beadworkers at Ska ru re. A long time before we migrated, the Maker of All Things had given us a special bird to be cared for by the young. As the story goes, we became lax, and the bird went away, and the time of our greatest struggles began. The bird is still with us, but it isn't. The people put the bird into the beads to help remember its message. Maybe that's why we hang onto our beadwork. My own affection for beads is like that of a potmaker for clay. Beads shaped my world, from the frivolous dangling jitterbugs to the intensely bead-laden sculptures.

Surrounded by a culture that seeks to smother our own, the beadwork is an island of memory in the fog. The face of my great-grandma next to the face of this beadwork is the face of our survival. Both have given me life, and that is how they are connected. It was not enough for me to bring a photograph from the past and give it words. I felt the need to put myself in the image. But isn't that what all artists do? In joining the beaded bird with berries and my great-grandma Flossie, I show how the berries feed the birds, the beads feed me and all the Ska ru re who walk the path of the "good mind." Cultures that adapt survive.

But to adapt does not mean that we must mimic the younger brother—the Euro-American. Cloaking ourselves in "Western" values has only meant trouble. This is why I make photographs. For us, the mask form is the face of protection, and photographs become the beads that cover my mask. They act as a thin veil between myself and the constant pressure to follow the path of destruction.

I consciously avoid slipping into the narrow language of response to the colonizers, who press up against us so hard. But I refuse to let them block my vision. My images reflect the Indian agenda. I am careful to remember that I have to pay just as much attention to the corn as I do to the chemical bath the sun sets in every day. The technology of photography is a dilemma I balance against the impact my work has on our threatened existence. I put my thoughts into the visual arts because they are meant to be felt, communicated. Writing and speaking are different acts, and they just don't do it for me. We survived by watching, listening, and experiencing life. A photograph is not going to give that firsthand experience, but it may haunt your memory into seeking life.

I recall the words of my father's brother, my uncle William: "Indians are the canaries of humankind. When we go, it's too late." On Turtle Island, known as North America, we make up less than five-tenths of one percent of the total population, with or without BIA species-enrollment numbers.[1]

My work is another bead on the cloth, visually linking our worldview to our experience. It is on our experience that I focus my eye, looking at the bits and pieces of our daily life while sorting through what belongs to us and what we picked up along the way. These images are not radically chic. I am just one Tuscarora woman who has identified the "center" as anywhere indigenous people continue to live, knowing that we have the oldest continuously surviving cultures in the world. That has to mean something. Every day I explore that meaning from the inside looking out.

Note:

1. Government-controlled tribal enrollment is a touchy issue in indigenous communities because it is imposed on our own ways of identifying each other. According to the old way, you inherited your nationhood and clan identity from your mother. In marriage, women stayed with their families and men moved into the women's families. The women were mostly in charge and possession of the material goods. Today some indigenous nations struggle to maintain control of who belongs with us, but the cataloguing of each indigenous birth by the U.S. government validates people who no longer understand the values which have sustained us since the beginning of time. At the same time it negates some who fall between the genealogical birthrights but do follow the path of the old ones, which is the path to the future. So the U.S. government continues to instigate our disappearance. For now, I fight with the barrel of my camera's lens.

Sources:

Interviews with Shirley Chew, Ska ru re Nation (1992); Lena Rickard, Ska ru re Nation (1991); Lucy Schubsta, Ska ru re Nation (1987). *The Tuscarora Legacy of J.N.B. Hewitt (J.N.B. Hewitt Wa? ekkirihwaye? O Ska ru re?)*, vol. 1 (Ottawa: Canadian Ethnographic Series 108, Canadian Museum of Civilization, National Museums of Canada, 1987).

Hulleah Tsinhnahjinnie, *Mattie Looks for Steve Biko*, photocollage, 1990.

(Courtesy Hulleah Tsinhnahjinnie.)

Gail Tremblay

REFLECTIONS ON

"MATTIE LOOKS FOR STEVE BIKO"

A Photograph by Hulleah Tsinhnahjinnie

Hulleah Tsinhnahjinnie is one of a number of important contemporary Native American photographers who alter or play with their images to create rich levels of metaphor and allusion.[1] Their images tell stories that reveal the human condition—informed, as it always is, by the context of culture, time, and place. I was first tempted to write about Jolene Rickard's work because we share roots in the Haudenosanee culture and her photographs often refer visually to our oral history, to our wampum belts, laws, customs, and traditions; seeing them is always like coming home. But I finally decided to write this essay on Mattie, Oakland, and Steve Biko. This particular image by Hulleah Tsinhnahjinnie has a history that resonates for me personally, politically, and spiritually.

To begin where this story begins for me: there are four sacred mountains that surround Navajo country. Hulleah's father, Andrew Tsinnajinnie,[2] was born among them, and that was where, in the 1920s, the agents of the United States tracked him down on the reservation to force him to go to a distant boarding school. Most teachers in Indian boarding schools in those days believed the children had to assimilate the values of European-American culture, and they not only wrenched Andrew Tsinnajinnie from his family, but they punished him for speaking his language and tried to make him disrespect the beliefs and culture of his people. Andrew, who missed his family very much and refused to do these things, ran away—first physically and then, when he was returned to the school, mentally.

Finally he moved to the Santa Fe Indian School and came upon a painting teacher who believed in the richness of his culture. He applied himself to his studies and became one of the most important Navajo painters of his generation,

113

able to support a large family by making art. In time he met the Creek/Seminole woman he married; she had had to leave her tribe because of lack of work in Oklahoma, where government removal had sent her people years before. Together their loving created Hulleah and her brothers and sisters. All this is very important in the development of Hulleah's vision of the world. She grew up in an environment where people were both affected by and refused to give in to oppression, and she had a model of the visual arts as a tool for survival, a way to celebrate the values of one's own culture.

The first time I saw one of Hulleah's photographs was in 1984 at the Silver Image Gallery in Seattle, in a traveling exhibition of Native American photographers curated by Jaune Quick-To-See Smith. I came upon Hulleah's photograph of Janeen Antoine in a white buckskin dress standing next to a motorcycle in San Francisco. It was a magic image that evoked for me something rarely expressed by the dominant European-American media about the nature of contemporary Native American life: we are twentieth-century people celebrating a culture that is as alive as we are. Here was this beautiful woman dressed for an urban powwow—that Indian institution that allows those relocated from homelands to urban centers by the government in the 1950s to express something important about who they are. There was a marvelous romanticism about this picture; yet it destroyed stereotypes by putting Indian people in a contemporary context and not freezing them in the past. I decided I wanted to meet the woman who made this photograph that had moved me deeply and made me feel less lonely.

I finally met Hulleah in 1985, at the opening of a mask exhibition at American Indian Contemporary Art in San Francisco. At the time she was on the board of that gallery, actively involved in both the Native American community and the Bay Area arts community. She had just made *The Metropolitan Indian Series Calendar* as a fund-raiser for the Intertribal Friendship House in Oakland, and I was very impressed and excited by the images of traditionally dressed indigenous people in urban settings—a further development of the first photograph I saw of hers. She juxtaposed the stark geometry of the Bay Area Rapid Transit stations and train cars against women in wing dresses and beaded bags with floral and animal designs, creating multileveled metaphors about who Native people are and where they belong. Although Hulleah was not yet using photocollage, it was clear that she was redefining reality. After seeing the calendar, I began to look forward to seeing more of Hulleah's work, trusting her to find ways to address complex issues and to challenge me, as a viewer, to think. I have never been disappointed—which brings us to *Mattie Looks for Steve Biko*.

In the mid-1980s, Hulleah began a series of photocollages, some of which focused on the image of "Mattie," a young Native girl whose family is originally from the Basin-Plateau of the Northwest. At least two years before I actually saw this photograph, Hulleah talked about it when we were discussing global politics and South Africa. Perhaps the conversation was sparked by something on the news; perhaps it was after I met Dennis Brutus, the South African poet/activist whose work I have always admired. In any case, Hulleah described a recent photocollage called *Mattie Looks for Steve Biko*. Mattie is seated on a Pendleton blanket in an old car wearing a wing dress and moccasins and looking out at the viewer. Behind her, visible through the car window, is an African-American family on their way to church on a sunny Sunday in Oakland. They seem comfortable, as though in a family snapshot, and they too look directly at the viewer. As we talked, I felt good that Hulleah and I shared a concern about racial injustice wherever it was. I was moved that she had chosen a Native child as the seeker of justice, with a black family to refer to racism against African-Americans in the U.S. and against native Africans in South Africa at the same time. When I finally saw the picture itself—in Hulleah's workroom, among other works in progress—I was not at all disappointed.

To put Hulleah's development into context, I want to talk a little about the history of art in Europe and among indigenous peoples in the United States. From the end of the Middle Ages until the late nineteenth century in Europe, most artists represented things they saw in their own environments and cultural milieus. During that period—roughly from the invention of perspective until the invention of the camera—good painting was that which created a two-dimensional illusion of reality. During this same period in North America—roughly from the arrival of Columbus to the beginning of the boarding school era—aesthetic work by indigenous people in the U.S. tended to be highly symbolic, often very abstract and conceptual in nature, and usually functional. Much of our aesthetic work was done to reflect our understanding of the spiritual nature of our way of life; often the most beautiful objects were used in ceremonial contexts, which were themselves highly aesthetic and spiritually powerful. It would be hard to imagine two groups of people with more different cultural and aesthetic values.

But after the invention of the camera, the aesthetic values of Europeans and U.S. indigenous people were inverted. The history of colonization and cross-cultural contact is the most important force in this change. The camera made a mechanical process of the creation of two-dimensional images that document reality, thus supplanting one of the functions of the artist in the Western cultural context. In

Europe, artists began to develop theories about the role of painting in relation to photography, and the most inventive artists began to move away from realism. Key to this break with traditions were the works of indigenous artists in Africa and the Pacific.

Colonization had permitted European anthropologists to collect "artifacts" or "material culture" and to create museums for them across the continent. European artists became fascinated with the power of these objects and used them to move their own art from representational to abstract and conceptual. This shift has been documented in art history books for most of the century, but always from a Euro-centric perspective that shows little respect for the arts of indigenous people around the globe. In the United States, at the time the camera was invented, European-Americans were still at war with indigenous nations. Some of the early photographic images of Native Americans documented the genocide that was taking place. For instance, there are photographs of Chief Bigfoot, dead and frozen in the snow, and of the mass grave after the massacre at Wounded Knee. Even after the wars had supposedly ended and the reservation period had begun, photographers continued to document the cultural genocide. While Edward Curtis was making romanticized pictures of "vanishing Americans," in an attempt to help us vanish, boarding schools were invented to force indigenous people to assimilate European ways, viewed as superior and "civilized" by the murderers of Indian people.

Our survival despite this period of intense violence and social upheaval testifies to the impossibility of eradicating Natives from the Mother Earth who supports us. Indian artists began to make drawings that documented their reality as a way to explain their cultures—each with its own beauty and values. First in the ledger-book drawings, stylistically based on the images on tipis, which showed a man's accomplishments as a hunter and soldier, and then in fine art, people began to re-present themselves to the world of outsiders, in their own terms.

This does not mean that Native Americans stopped making traditional aesthetic work; one need only look around an American Indian community today to see such work everywhere, functioning as it should. It means that ever since the late nineteenth century, some indigenous artists have found it important to paint and sculpt with reverence about who their ancestors were and about the beauty of their way of life. These artists found the need to develop art with a new function: to proclaim their humanity and their right to survive as peoples. Some countered present oppression with lovingly romantic evocations of the past.

Euro-American writers have made much of the fact that the art teachers in the boarding schools were white, and the market addressed was also white. They have talked too little to the artists themselves about the importance of finding a way to do something that celebrated Native culture, asserted one's beauty and humanity in a world that was always denying it, and preserved the stories told by the grandparents one loved, from whom one was taken. Missionaries were telling people that their ceremonies were primitive and uncivilized, banning the sacred beings and tricksters that made life rich and allowed indigenous people to bear the unbearable. White writers failed to understand the need of Indian people to speak about these things—not only in their own communities, where they were being taught to internalize negative messages about themselves, but also in the dominating community, where some enlightened European-Americans were trying to convince their own people that there was value in Native culture. This is the world into which Andrew Tsinnajinnie was born in 1916. As an artist, he responded to it by creating representational artwork that celebrated the beauty and harmony of the Navajo world in the face of a hostile outside world that devalued it. He used his art to preserve a reality, to support his own and other indigenous children, so that the people and culture could carry on.

One of the ironies of the inversion in aesthetic values after the invention of photography (in which European art became more abstract and Native American art became more realistic) is that it has caused the elite in Western culture to marginalize the art of contemporary Native American artists—this time because the art is not abstract. Some artists of Andrew Tsinnajinnie's generation, most notably Oscar Howe, responded by creating highly symbolic and abstract art which visually paralleled that of the Euro-American mainstream, despite its very different sources. But generally it has been the next generation of artists who have moved toward the abstract and conceptual, searching the aesthetic and spiritual values of their pasts for a way to speak to their generation about the Native world.

Hulleah Tsinhnahjinnie was born from her father's tradition into this contemporary Native American art world with its multifaceted pressures on the artist to fit others' definitions of what it is to be an indigenous person and artist. Initially, she trained as a painter and was given negative criticism whenever she painted representational or romantic images that developed stylistically from the work of her father's generation. This criticism was often delivered in a culturally insensitive way, but it did lead Hulleah to explore photography as another representational medium with which to address her concerns. Given the history I have outlined above, there is a wonderful paradox in her choice of the camera, which helped speed radical change in European painting and was in turn used in such offensive ways to depict Native American communities.

Hulleah met the pressures to transcend realism in her art by making work that speaks directly to this postmodern world about ways to live in harmony, or, as

Hulleah's Navajo ancestors might say, to walk in beauty. By using collage and layering images, she has been able to subvert the documentary nature of her medium and challenge the reality of the dominating American culture. She forces the viewer to confront indigenous people as important subjects in the contemporary world. At the same time, her constant references to tradition and traditional clothing allow her to maintain her father's celebration of culture and to assault the world that tries to tell us we are vanishing. She constructs new images by layering and often rephotographing old ones, putting them in new contexts. As a photographer, Hulleah not only documents the events of the Native world, she positions Natives in the world.

I saw *Mattie Looks for Steve Biko* again in Oakland in 1990, at an exhibition called "Talking Drum, Connected Vision: Native American Artists Addressing Affinities with the Indigenous People of South Africa." The show was organized by the multicultural artists' group Salad Bar, to commemorate Nelson Mandela's visit to Oakland and his promise to return and talk with Native people and the world about the treatment of indigenous people in the Americas. Hulleah chose this image of Steve Biko, who was not a member of the African National Congress. He is, however, a powerful example to indigenous people who understand the importance of decolonizing the mind and undoing the effects of internalized oppression, because of his interest in issues of history and African culture.

I was startled to see that the image had changed. Hulleah had added one more element, framing the original photocollage in a television set, so that it appeared as a picture on the screen. This added another level of irony. I began to have fantasies about Mattie directly addressing the American public about racial injustice through the media, interviewing this African-American family in Oakland about their lives and about Steve Biko. I imagined a world where Native people shaped media and defined the subjects and perspectives that deserved attention. Mattie looked directly into the camera and told America the things it most needed to hear. This contemporary American Indian girl, in her youth and beauty, dressed in the outfit in which she celebrates her culture, dances, goes to the longhouse and makes ceremony live, discovers the injustice done to African people on two continents. Given the way American media has historically created stereotypes and controlled images of people of color, the irony is overwhelming and, at the same time, liberating.

In the catalogue for "Talking Drum," Hulleah wrote:

While in high school on the rez, I would sit in the library looking at pictures. . . . I happened upon a book titled House of Bondage. *The images were incredible. I sat and cried. I compared the living conditions of Native Americans to South Africans which in turn began my questioning . . . "why?"*

It is this ability to empathize with others' pain and to oppose injustice wherever she sees it that draws me to Hulleah's art. That and the beauty of indigenous culture that shines forth from everything she does. She creates images that speak both aesthetically and politically about a postcolonial reality where each person is the subject of their own story, with a valid relationship to all the other stories being told. This photograph is not about assimilation or the creation of a monoculture; it is about parallel realities that claim respect and speak to the whole world about the need to end exploitation and oppression. On a planet with a history that makes me shudder, where peace is still possible if we act lovingly for Earth to support life, this photograph is a song sung with great grace. The world is at this moment richer if we choose to understand the multiple levels of its implications.

Notes:

1. Others who do this include Carm Little Turtle, Joe Feddersen, Larry McNeil, Jesse Cooday, and Pena Bonita. It was difficult to choose one image from among all those created by these artists, because I am drawn to each one's work.
2. Father and daughter spell their names differently.

Sarah Penman, *Wounded Knee, 1989.* (Courtesy Sarah Penman.)

David Seals

Sarah Penman has titled her black-and-white photograph simply *Wounded Knee, 1989*, but those words and the date say a lot about it. These are today's Indians, survivors of five hundred years of horror in this hemisphere, and you can see part of the reason for the survival in their faces, their angry defiant eyes. These are the Lakotas of South Dakota, better known to the world as the Sioux, and they are not "Friendlies" like some other tribes around the continent who tried to get along with the European invaders in a peaceful way. These are the "Hostiles" of Sitting Bull and Crazy Horse, the ferocious kickers of Custer's ass at the Little Bighorn River, the victims of the equally ferocious Germans and English at Wounded Knee.

But that's all history, you might say, and these are today's Indians. Yet the history is still very much a part of Celene Not Help Him, an Oglala elder from the Pine Ridge reservation. She may be wearing a ratty Salvation Army coat and scarf, a typical poverty outfit in the poorest county of the U.S.A., her face probably older than her years. I don't know her age, but I know these people. I live in South Dakota too, and this photo is stinky real, these people are cold and probably haven't eaten much lately. Poverty is a wild angry frustrating daily anguish of worrying about finding something to eat, to feed the children, to find gas money to get to the store that may be miles away, or to get to a friend's to borrow food or money, or to town to beg for food stamps or an AFDC check that's late. The humiliation of poverty is behind their angry faces. The wealth of tourists who come to the Black Hills and Mount Rushmore is obscene. They cruise around in fifty-thousand-dollar recreational vehicles and Cadillacs and eat nice meals in expensive restaurants, while Indian children in my neighborhood of Rapid City tell me they haven't eaten all day.

They come to me, families in old, beat-up vans and cars, asking for twenty dollars to get home, to get something to eat. Sometimes I have it and sometimes I don't. I don't have a car myself, and I have two children to raise. I live in a predominantly Indian neighborhood of north Rapid, not far from the instant mini-ghetto of Lakota Homes: rows of plain government housing with no trees, separated from the nice (white) residential area of west Rapid City where these desperate brown faces are noticeably missing. Over there you see nice cars on the roads, clean parks, shopping centers. In north Rapid it's mainly old wrecks on the roads and in the backyards, a lot of old people walking from the Safeway with a sack or two of groceries, wild sleezy bars where people are stabbed frequently. You go by those places and Indians are out in the parking lot, screaming at each other beside their wrecks. Winos wander through the parks here, sour staggering joking hopeless drunks, sitting under the bridges, panhandling the yuppie bicyclists who cruise through quickly on the bike path.

There is a perverse integrity in these winos. They refuse to join the American system. They will not get jobs and be "responsible," which of course infuriates many Americans. They'd rather die than become like the hated deceivers of their ancestors, the American violators of the peace treaties. They do not forget, nor forgive—for they have told me under the bridges, in the words of one tall, slim, fullblood man with long black hair, "You have not said you're sorry for what you do to us. So how can we forgive you?" That question is also in the eyes of people in this photograph.

I know Sarah Penman, and she knows the poverty too. She was here this summer (1991) to do a vision quest on the sacred mountain in the Black Hills, Bear Butte, and her old, beat-up car broke down. She had no money to fix it and was trying to sell her pictures, without much luck. Then her car rolled down into a gulley, I guess the brake wasn't too good, and it was totalled. It was a typical Indian experience. When I bought this photo from her for $30, she was absolutely devastated and destitute. She sold the old wreck to get another one, for $400, and needed my money to fix the voltage regulator, I think it was. She was deep in a 1965 Ford engine, and various mechanics experienced in these old bombers were trying to help her. She was up to her elbows in grease and anger and despair. She was getting a good feel for her subject matter in that rusty old machine on a hot South Dakota afternoon.

Sarah is from Scotland and has been living in Minneapolis, not far from the western Teton Sioux territory which seems to be her favorite subject matter. She has come here frequently, to ride with the Wounded Knee Riders in the December sub-zero re-creation of the hideous ride in 1890 that led to the Wounded Knee massacre. They start from Sitting Bull's home on the Grand River, near the North Dakota border, where he was assassinated by drunken Indian Police under orders from the president of the United States, and they ride 150 miles over the stark prairie terrain of buttes and thin creeks, across the eerie sandy moonscape of the Badlands, and down south almost to the Nebraska border, where Red Cloud's Oglalas were huddling in terror and starvation in 1890. Sarah has epic shots of the riders on the snowswept plains, where the wind chill has been forty below the last few Decembers and frostbite was not uncommon. Hundreds of men and women brave our terrible winter to make their symbolic homage to their dead ancestors. The media come from all over for the picturesque shots, but few of them ride along as Sarah has. She puts up with the lousy sparse food around the freezing campfires. She struggles to find a blanket or a friend in the night, a warm place to sleep, a hot drink.

She puts up with prejudice. She photographs the holy man of the Sioux—Arvol Looking Horse, the Keeper of the Sacred Pipe of White Buffalo Woman, the Goddess who founded their culture and brought the Seven Ceremonies (Sweat Lodge, Vision Quest, etc.)—and is criticized by others for taking his picture. There are many self-appointed Lakotas who are keepers of their own pure flames, in their own minds, who love to play bad-ass Indian around white people, especially white women. They've given her a lot of shit, that she shouldn't photograph Arvol when he's praying. Arvol himself doesn't object, but these other guys think they know better. Racism and sexism are big problems in Indian country, and Sarah has captured that too in her photographs.

Sure, there are a lot of white people who are ripping off Indian culture for their own profit and the Indians don't see a dime. It's a legitimate grievance. Happy New Agers in California are making fortunes on the Lakota spirituality while Arvol and the other true medicine men are living in hovels. Hollywood loves to come around and play out their fantasies, never once stopping to feed an Indian child or give a grandmother like Celene Not Help Him $50 for food and gas. These movie companies come in here all the time and spend millions of dollars flogging their fantasies of the Noble Savage. Indians are justly suspicious.

If many whites are hated by many Indians, and vice versa, women are doubly discriminated against. Women are not included in traditional Councils. White women are, in the words of Judy Merritt, a white woman I know, "third-class citizens." At a recent Elders Council, the men all sat in the shade of a tipi and had a big important meeting, while the women served them coffee and drinks and had to sit outside in the broiling summer sun. The Indian women further lorded it over the white women who were there in all sincerity to learn and help. Merritt added,

"All they did was gossip and bitch. If women were included more in these things, they wouldn't come off so bad. They'd have just as much to say and add."

How Sarah got this photograph must be viewed from this background, off camera. I don't think these three people wanted this white woman to take their picture, especially not up so close. Indians are used to people coming around all the time wanting to take their pictures, and they laugh about it, scorn it. It's a real disinterested cultural detachment, a bad habit of many Americans toward other cultures, "foreigners." But Sarah got right in there, anyway. So what, they're mad at me, this picture says. Show me your anger, because that is righteous and beautiful too.

And they have played it for all it's worth. Next to Celene is Robert Sierra, who, Sarah laughed when I asked her about him, "was in jail last I heard." That says even more about the sociopolitics bursting from his magnificent stare. There is intelligence in his defiance too, the physical strength and beauty of the men which I'm sure has also drawn Sarah to these rich emotional badlands. White women seem to be around all the time, sexually attracted to the tall, handsome Sioux. And, unfortunately, they often leave embittered and confused after a few wild and furtive relationships. But several women have told me they also leave impressed with the men's intelligence. A high percentage of the Lakota are indeed impressively smart. They can talk about history and treaties with their famous oratory, passionate about their spirituality and often able to express it in fine poetic phrases, especially in the Lakota language. It's a powerful culture, and that shows in the photograph. But even more, I see the less savory truths here.

Robert Sierra's life reflects social and racial injustice, the onus of history hanging over him; the anguish and desperation of poverty. But there is also what Mary Crow Dog described in her book *Lakota Woman*—the egotism, the deep sexism of Sioux men. His is a macho expression, that of a man like those Mary described as wife-beaters and rapists. I'm not saying Robert Sierra is either, but his is a typical grimace of too much pride, and maybe more than enough ignorance about whites and women and other cultures as well. Alcoholism is a despicable failing, a childish fault, and it is epidemic here. The image of this man is an allegory of the machismo, the alcoholic chauvinism, the rural narrow-mindedness that has always weakened the Lakotas. Sitting Bull was murdered by his own drunken relatives, but today their descendants rant and rave endlessly about needing new leaders like Sitting Bull. Why, so they can kill such a man or woman too? I am speaking brutally here, but I am only telling what I see in this brutal photograph of the truth inside South Dakota today.

It is good that these truths are photographed. Maybe the Lakotas can grow up. I have learned living here that they are much more receptive to constructive criticism than mainstream Americans.

The smooth transition to the third figure in the photograph, Ron McNeil, is, thematically at least, fitting, as he is a descendant of Sitting Bull. He is also posing to some extent. They all know they're being photographed. Sierra is holding a flagpole or a lance in some semiofficial position, perhaps. Sarah called this picture the "Mount Rushmore shot." The three are captured in a marching frame, looking off in three different directions, like the four presidents carved into the Black Hills. But they are not cozy and comfortable, secure in their world, like Washington and Jefferson and Lincoln and Roosevelt. For these three Indians it's cold outside. Ron McNeil's sunglasses say that it is probably a bright white sunny snowy day. All he and Robert Sierra have to cover their ears is their long black hair, hanging loosely, aggressively uncut and unbraided. No fancy ribbons and beadwork here. No secure niches and cozy worlds for these three.

Sarah has captured the edge where warriors live, the brink of death and ruin hanging over everyone all the time, but only warriors are consciously aware of it and live with it at all times. Celene is probably the toughest of the three, having lived through the hell of poverty and racism and sexism longer. Elders are grudgingly respected because they have somehow survived all the shit. There is a mystique about them, a sacredness about modern Indians like these, for all their faults and ferocity. Indians are damn tough and I love them, as Sarah obviously does too. I like this photo because it has none of the glamor or romance New Agers seem so infatuated with. There are no easy and fun arts and crafts at work here. Only raw elements blowing around these people, politics and economics, which scare yuppies and filmmakers. Not one goddamn ounce of sentimentality.

PHOTOGRAPHS

Information on most of these photographs is sparse, to say the least, and the emphasis in this context, as noted in the introduction, is visual rather than scholarly. The "quaint" captions are the originals, often handwritten on front or back of photographs. Negative numbers, when known, follow the sources.

Frederick Starr, *La Pinta*, Silao, Mexico, 1896. (NMAI/SI 18035.)

M. R. Harrington, *Horns Devil Dancer Showing Use of Mask,* Chiricahua Apache, near
Lawton, Okla., 1909. (NMAI/SI 2860.)

H. S. Poley, *Hopi Runner*, Walpi, August 1899. (DPL/WHC P738.) Handwritten on back of photo: "Just at sunrise on the morning of the 9th day of the Snake Dance ceremony the young men have a great race from far in the valley to the pueblo. The first arrival at the top of the trail."

Nancy Wood, *Frank Marcus, Jr., Chases His Wife, Juana, During a Water Fight at Eliseo Concha's Ranch*. (From Nancy Wood, *Taos Pueblo*, [New York: Alfred A. Knopf, 1989]; Courtesy Nancy Wood.)

Alfred M. Bailey, *Old Man Dancing in Wainwright School House,* 1921. (Courtesy Denver Museum of Natural History.) Bailey, a museum naturalist who later became the director of the Denver Museum of Natural History, worked in Alaska from 1919 to 1922, living in the arctic village and trading post of Wainwright on the Chukchi Sea in 1921–22. During the midwinter weeks of darkness, the Inuit population danced, feasted, and visited. This photo was probably taken on January 26, when dances at the schoolhouse welcomed the return of the sun.

J. D. Leechman, *Duwamish (Snoqualmie) Spirit Canoe Ceremony,* Tolt, King County, Wash., 1920. (NMAI/SI 6757.) "Lifting Over the Daylight" was part of the Spirit Canoe Ceremony, "reenacted to recover the lost soul of a dead patient. The ritual depicted [the] journey of the shamans to [the] land of the dead to recover the body" (Joanna Cohan Scherer).

Wheeler Expedition, *Navajo*, 1873. (CHS F21069.)

William C. Orchard, *Chaco Canyon, Old George's Family,* October 1900. (NMAI/SI 3758.) The presence of the white woman and child on the other side of the barbed wire from the Navajo family gives this picture a double edge. A second attribution credits Sumner Matteson with this photograph, and dates it 1899.

Apache Meal. (CHS, from glass negative.) The beautiful Pueblo pot near the burned-out cooking fire and tin can may have been the photographer's addition, although in this context it seems unlikely.

Susan Russell (John Russell's wife and Edna Baker's Mother), Bessie Box (little girl),
Sally Box, Bessie Tobias, Ute. (CHS F15456.)

De Cost Smith, *Omaha Woman and Children,* Omaha Reservation, Nebr., 1892.
(NMAI/SI 22440.) Although both children are dressed in "white" clothes, the one
on the left appears to be Native, while the baby could be European. The unnamed
woman may have been married to a white man.

Inspection of Camp, Hunkpapa Sioux. (NMAI/SI 38012.)

Inspection of Camp, Hunkpapa Sioux. (NMAI/SI 38012.)

Joseph Keppler, *Masked Men at Sacrifice of White Dog Ceremony,* Seneca, Cattaraugus
Reservation, N.Y., 1905. (NMAI/SI 36798.) The dog strangled on pole at the left was

part of a New Year's feast.

Edward H. Davis, *Dance at Girl's Puberty Ceremony,* Diegueño, Mesa Grande, Calif.,
1931. (NMAI/SI 25643.)

Jesse Nusbaum, *Indians Excavating Pecos Pueblo*, New Mexico. (DPL/WHC 7162.)

Kopsicha near Tipi in Winter, Sioux, Devil's Lake Reservation, N.D., c. 1892.
(Presented by John H. Waugh, NMAI/SI 20159.)

Indian Girl Scouts out for a Summer Trip near the Reservation, Ute, Ignacio Reservation, Colo. (CHS F41916.) The scouts hold hot dogs on very long sticks—the irony of teaching Indian children to cook outdoors. Handwritten on back of the photo: "L to R: 6th one, Arbella Williams, 10th Ruby Taylor, 11th Vida Baker Peabody."

G. W. Ingalls (?), *Graduation Class of 1875*, Cherokee Young Ladies Seminary,
Park Hill, Indian Territory, Okla. (DPL/WHC F45771.) Handwritten on back of
photo: "Cost $45,000. Built by the Tribe without U.S. Government aid. Fruits of
Christian Civilization."

H. S. Poley, *Hopi Children Playing.* (DPL/WHC P1099.)

William Stiles, *Nascapi Indian Children Playing*, Davis Inlet, Labrador, Newfoundland, Canada, June 1965. (NMAI/SI 33329.)

Daisy Eagle (Ellen H. Watts' Mother) and Child, Ute. (CHS F41882.)

Fred R. Meyer, *Chee-Toc-Tei-Toc*, Crow, Reno District, Mont., c. 1903.
(NMAI/SI 22073.)

Sumner Matteson, *Painter F. P. Sauerwein Sketching Francisco, the Governor of Santa Clara Pueblo,* New Mexico, 1900. (Courtesy Milwaukee Public Museum.) Taken with a No. 3 Folding Pocket Kodak camera. Another photograph taken of the same scene earlier in the day indicates how the photographer has rearranged the environment here for compositional reasons. Frank Paul Sauerwein (1871–1910) went to the Southwest in 1891, lived at Hopi, and traveled in New Mexico and Arizona. He died at thirty-nine and his ashes were scattered in the Painted Desert.

Nancy Wood, *Uncle John Concha Tries on His Traditional Blanket.* "John Concha is a small man, not over five feet four, slightly built, but with the power to swing an ax at the age of eighty-five. His long braids are wrapped around his head like a turban. On his feet he wears a pair of moccasins so old that they have turned black with years of use. . . . He used to be a runner, he says, but this was not like the jogging of today. It was simply a way for a man to be in contact with the earth, to echo its rhythm, to unite flesh with earth, to encourage the earth for the sake of the whole village." (From Nancy Wood, *Taos Pueblo* [New York: Alfred A. Knopf, 1989]; Courtesy Nancy Wood.)

H. S. Poley, *Hopi Boy Weaving,* Walpi. (DPL/WHC P98.) Label on front reads:
"Weaving prayer rug in deserted kiva or cave, Moki Indians . . ."

George Byrd Grinnell, *Cheyenne Woman Carrying Child*, Lame Deer, Mont.
(NMAI/SI 13538.) The photographer was Edward Curtis's mentor, an anthropologist
who was also editor of *Forest and Stream* magazine. He was called "Fisher Hat" by the
Blackfeet and Piegan.

Kate Cory, *Division of Old Oraibi,* 1906. (Courtesy Museum of Northern Arizona, Flagstaff, MS208 #89.383, Kate Cory Collection.) "Thereupon, the Friendlies set about clearing the village of Shungopovis. They began at the very spot where they stood; but every Friendly who laid hold of a Shungopovi to put him out of doors was attacked from behind by an Oraibi Hostile, so that the three went wrestling and struggling out of doors together." (Helen Sekaquaptewa, *Me and Mine,* [Tucson: University of Arizona Press, 1989]). This photo is the only known documentation of the atypically belligerent split between Hopis who were friendly toward whites and those who were hostile. Kate Thompson Cory studied art at the Cooper Union in New York, heard about the Hopi mesas from a painter friend, and at the age of forty-four went there to live with the people at Oraibi and Walpi for seven years, painting and photographing, developing her negatives with rainwater. She was invited into the kivas, where even Hopi women were not allowed. "Why they accepted her with such grace is a mystery." (Marnie Gaede, *The Hopi Photographs: Kate Cory 1905–1912* [Albuquerque: University of New Mexico Press, 1986].) No one knows why she left the mesas, or how she supported herself. Cory settled in Prescott, Arizona, poor and eccentric, still visited by Hopi friends. She died in 1958.

Frank Churchill, *Zunis with Superintendent D. D. Graham.* Zuni Pueblo, 1906.
(NMAI/SI 26726.) A rare image of an actual interchange between Native and white people.

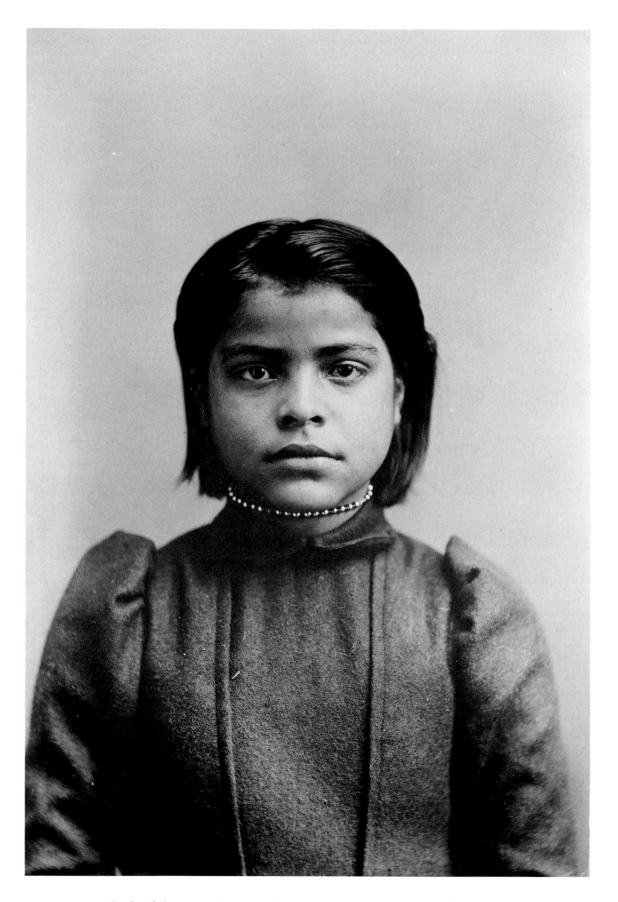

Frederick Starr, *Ada Brenninger,* Chippewa, Haskell Institute. (NMAI/SI 15369.)
Haskell Institute, in Lawrence, Kansas, was an Indian boarding school.

Goes Up Hill, Arapaho. (DPL/WHC F39683.)

Goes Up Hill, Arapaho. (DPL/WHC F39683.)

De Cost Smith, *Crow Reservation, Montana,* 1890. (NMAI/SI 37136.)

Frederick Starr, *Women's Football*, Iroquois, Newtown, N.Y., 1894–1910. (NMAI/SI 15302.)   159

Osage Women, Pawhuska, Okla., 1899. (NMAI/SI 27187.)

Edward H. Davis, *Death Image Ceremony*, Luiseño, Pala, Calif., 1904.
(NMAI/SI 24354.)

Zerviah Mitchell, Wampanoag, Mass., 1872. (NMAI/SI 15198.)

Mrs. Zerviah Gould Mitchell, Wampanoag, Lakeville, Mass. (NMAI/SI 12258.)
Zerviah Mitchell, seventh generation descendant of Chief Massasaoit, great-
granddaughter of Lydia Tuspaquin, was born July 24, 1807, and died in 1899.

Charles Rau, *Tlingit Women Trading,* Treadwell, Alaska. (NMAI/SI 36412.)

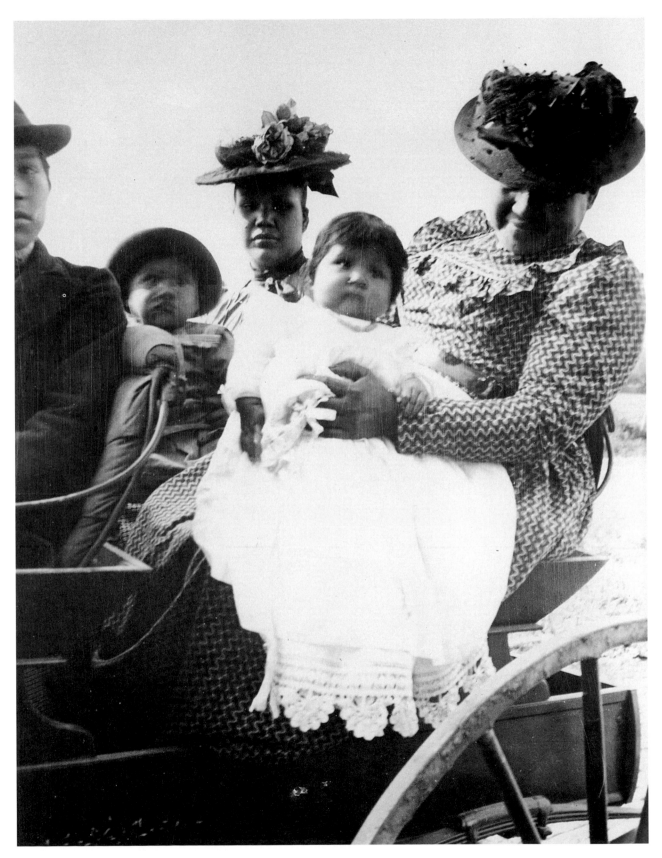

Gerry Jones and Family in Carriage, Seneca, Cattaraugus Reservation, N.Y., c. 1900.
(NMAI/SI 23085.)

Ute Men Playing Cards. (CHS 10575.)

Frank Matsura, *A Cowboy Named Barrett and Paul "Long Paul" Timentwa, A Colville Rancher.* (Courtesy Okanogan County Historical Society, Okanogan, Wash.)

Gertrude Käsebier, *Untitled Portrait of Indians Accompanying Buffalo Bill's Wild West Show.* (Library of Congress, 86-2205.) Although the soft-focus pictorialism may have romanticized the subjects, the direct gazes dispel illusions. Käsebier (1852–1934) grew up near Denver, moved to New York in her teens, but only began photographing when her three children were grown. In 1898, she established a portrait studio on Fifth Avenue, and was a member of the Photo-Secession group with Stieglitz and Steichen.

Harriet Smith Pullen, *Mrs. Stene-Tu, a Tlinget* [sic] *Belle*, 1906. (reproduced by permission from *Native American Portraits*, by Nancy Hathaway [San Francisco: Chronicle Books, 1990].) The classic postcard shot; women photographers were not immune.

Ben Wittick, *A Dying Mojave.* (Courtesy Museum of New Mexico, Santa Fe, 16,237). The Mojaves' religious beliefs centered on the acquisition of power by dreams and on mourning ceremonies at death.

Horace Poolaw (Kiowa), *Kaw-au-in-on-tay and Great-grandson Jerry Poolaw*, Mountain View, Okla., c. 1928. (Courtesy Linda Poolaw and Stanford University Humanities Center.) Kaw-au-in-on-tay was captured in the 1840s from Sonora, Mexico, as a twelve-year-old girl with her two sisters, and remained with the Kiowa. According to Linda Poolaw, Kaw-au-in-on-tay's brother spotted the Kiowa encampment several days after his sisters were kidnapped, and found the tipi they were held in. He told them he'd be back at night with horses to rescue them. He did come, and her two sisters went with him, but at the last minute she got scared and stayed behind. She was probably born in the 1820s. This picture was taken when she was approximately one hundred years old. (Letter from Charles Junkerman, May 8, 1992). 171

Gerald Vizenor (Chippewa), *Anishinabe Burial Ceremony; Daniel Raincloud, with Rattle, near Coffin Bearing the Body of John Ka Ka Geesick,* Warroad, Minn., 1968. (Courtesy Gerald Vizenor.) John Ka Ka Geesick was an Anishinabe shaman who died at the age of 124, having lived most of his life as a trapper and woodsman on Muskeg Bay. His name was derived from *gaagige giizhig*—"forever" and "day," or "everlasting day." He was, writes Vizenor, "known to tourists because he had posed for a photograph from which postcards were printed and sold. He was invented and colonized in the photograph, pictured in a blanket and turkey-feather headdress. On the streets of the town he wore common clothes. . . . He was a town treasure, in a sense, an image from the tribal past, but when he died the mortician dressed him in a blue suit, with a white shirt and necktie." Daniel Raincloud is a healer and shaman from Ponemah on the Red Lake Reservation. This traditional burial ceremony, held in the school gymnasium, was followed by a Christian service in which "a white evangelist delivered a passionate eulogy about a man he had never seen inside his church" (*The People Named the Chippewa,* Minneapolis: University of Minnesota Press, 1976).

Kate Cory, *A Hopi Man Carries a Dead Infant to the Cemetery,* c. 1905–12. (Courtesy Museum of Northern Arizona, Flagstaff MS208 #75:967, Kate Cory Collection.)

Frank G. Speck, *Wife of Mitchell Buckshot in Native Costume,* Desert River Algonkin,
Quebec, Canada, 1927. (NMAI/SI 13073.)

Frank Matsura, *Cecile Joe.* (Courtesy Okanogan County Historical Society, Okanogan, Wash.)
She wears two brooches of framed photographs, apparently of white men.

Ford-Bartlett Expedition, *Eskimos in Kayaks*, Angmagssalik, East Greenland, 1930.
(NMAI/SI 36485.)

Frank G. Speck, *Bark Canoe*, Penobscot, Indian Island, Maine, 1924.
(NMAI/SI 12979.)

M. R. Harrington, *August Williams, Turkey Clan, and Jacob Robinson, Wildcat Clan,*
Kosati, Houma, La., 1908. (NMAI/SI 2739; 2738.) The old man was a doctor.
Perhaps the flowers and the book refer to his or their professions?

Monument to Chief Ouray and Chipeta. (DPL/WHC F23417.) This unveiling probably took place in western Colorado in the 1920s or 1930s. Ouray was the great Ute chief who, nevertheless, presided over his nation's loss of most of its territory. Chipeta, his wife, was also his partner, and went everywhere with him. After his death, she was exiled to an arid reservation in Utah. The flag-veiled phallic form seems an ironic commemoration.

Mile High Photo Studio, *Crow Indian Tribe from Montana,* Denver, Colo., 1930s (?).
(CHS 33739.)

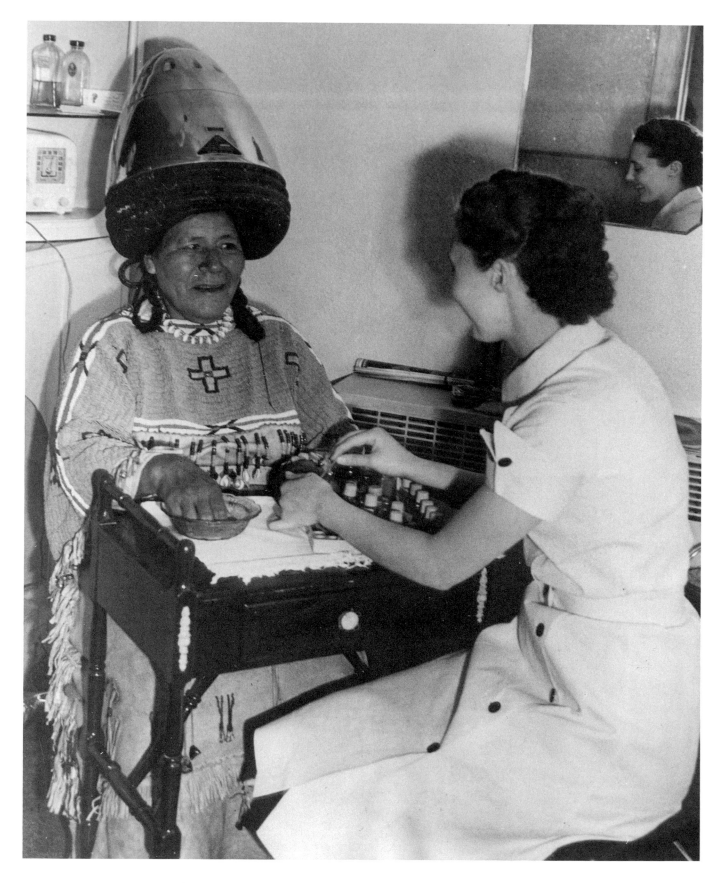

Red Cloud Woman in Beauty Shop, Dakota, 1941. (DPL/WHC F24181.) Labeled on back
of photo: "Assimilation."

Helen M. Post, *Their Store Shows a Steady Profit,* Jicarilla Apache tribal co-op store,
New Mexico, c. 1940. (From Oliver LaFarge, *As Long as the Grass Shall Grow,*
[New York: Longmans Green & Co., 1940].)

Picuris Indians' Deer Dance Float in Southern Ute Fair Parade. (DPL/WHC F24719.) The float, simulating a sacred dance, won a prize. A second label on the photo says this was designed by two southern Ute tribes.

Paul Chaat Smith (Comanche), *Yankton Sioux Reservation, 1976* (Courtesy Paul Chaat Smith).   185

Interior of Kiva Showing Murals, Zuni, New Mexico, 1906. (NMAI/SI 26755, Churchill Collection.)

Don Doll, *Interior of Julia Kills in Sight's Home,* 1987. (Courtesy Don Doll.) The resistance poster "We Remember Wounded Knee" hangs with family military photographs and artistic objects, and counters a plate reproduction of James Frazier's
discouragingly famous sculpture *End of the Trail*.

Wovoka, Paiute Prophet of the Ghost Dance Religion, and General Tim McCoy, Hollywood Cowboy Actor, on location for a western film near Walker Lake Reservation, Nev., 1926. (Courtesy National Anthropological Archives, Smithsonian Institution 1659-C.) McCoy was later governor of Wyoming Territory.

John Running, *Redwing Nez and Son,* 1991. (Courtesy John Running.) Nez is Navajo, a contemporary movie actor, singer, and painter.

Kathleen Westcott (White Earth Ojibwe), *Amy White Man Runs Him Braiding Her*
Hair, Lodge Grass, Mont., 1979. (Courtesy Kathleen Westcott.)

Richard Hill (Tuscarora/Mohawk), *The Flowered Path: On the Way to My Brother's Funeral,* 1971. (Courtesy Richard Hill.)

Al Abrams, *Public Drinking, Phoenix, Arizona,* 1990, from "The Urban Indian" series.
(Courtesy Abrams Photo/Graphics, Phoenix.)

Sam Bingham, *Katherine Smith with Rifle She Used to Resist Relocation at Big Mountain.*
(Courtesy Sam Bingham.)

David Neel (Kwakiutl), *Chief/Reverend Charlie Swanson and Photographer David Neel,*
1990. (Courtesy David Neel.) From a series called "Our Chiefs and Elders."

Alinder, Jim and Don Doll, eds., *Crying for a Vision: A Rosebud Sioux Trilogy 1886–1976*, Dobbs Ferry, N.Y.: Morgan and Morgan, 1976.

Ralph W. Andrews, *Indian Primitive*, New York: Bonanza Books, 1960.

Baker, Will, *Backward: An Essay on Indians, Time, and Photography*, Berkeley: North Atlantic Books, 1983.

Belous, Russell E. and Robert A. Weinstein, *Will Soule: Indian Photographer at Fort Sill, Oklahoma 1869–74*, Los Angeles: The Ward Ritchie Press, 1969.

Broder, Patricia Janis, *Shadows on Glass: The Indian World of Ben Wittick*, Savage, Md.: Rowman and Littlefield Publishers, 1990.

Carpenter, Edmund, *Oh, What a Blow That Phantom Gave Me!*, New York: Holt, Rinehart and Winston, 1972.

Casagrande, Louis B. and Phillip Bourns, *Side Trips: The Photography of Sumner W. Matteson 1898–1908*, Milwaukee: Milwaukee Public Museum; and The Science Museum of Minnesota.

Collier, John Jr., *Visual Anthropology: Photography as a Research Method*, New York: Holt, Rinehart and Winston, 1967.

Farr, William, *The Reservation Blackfeet 1882–1945, A Photographic History of Cultural Survival*, Seattle: University of Washington Press, 1984. (Introduction by James Welch.)

Fleming, Paula Richardson and Judith Luskey, *The North American Indians in Early Photographs*, New York: Dorset Press, 1988.

Harrison, Julia, *Métis: People Between Two Worlds*, Vancouver/Toronto: The Glenbow-Alberta Institute and Douglas & McIntyre, 1985.

Hathaway, Nancy, *Native American Portraits*, San Francisco: Chronicle Books, 1990.

Lyman, Christopher, *The Vanishing Race and Other Illusions: Photographs of Indians by Edward S. Curtis*, New York: Pantheon Books, Washington, D.C.: Smithsonian Institution Press, 1982.

McLuhan, T. C., *Dream Tracks: The Railroad and the American Indian 1890–1930*, New York: Harry N. Abrams, 1985.

Masayesva, Victor and Erin Younger, eds., *Hopi Photographers/Hopi Images*, Tucson: Sun Tracks and University of Arizona Press, 1983.

Roe, Jo Ann, *Frank Matsura: Frontier Photographer*, Seattle: Madrona Publishers, 1981.

Scherer, Joanna Cohan, *Indians: The Great Photographs That Reveal North American Indian Life, 1874–1929, from the Unique Collection of the Smithsonian Institution*, New York: Crown Publishers, 1973.

Scherer, Joanna Cohan, "You Can't Believe Your Eyes: Inaccuracies in Photographs of North American Indians," *Exposure*, Winter, 1978.

Silko, Leslie Marmon, *Storyteller*, New York: Little Brown and Company, 1981.

Viola, Herman, *North American Indians: Photographs from the National Anthropological Archives of the Smithsonian Institution*, Chicago: University of Chicago Press, 1974.

Vizenor, Gerald, *Crossbloods: Bone Courts, Bingo and Other Reports*, Minneapolis: University of Minnesota Press, 1976/1990.

Webb, William and Robert A. Weinstein, *Dwellers at the Source: Southwestern Indian Photographs of A.C. Vroman, 1895–1904*, New York: Grossman, 1973.

Nancy Wood, *Taos Pueblo*, New York: Alfred A. Knopf, 1989.

Wright, Barton, Marnie Gaede and Marc Gaede, *The Hopi Photographs, Kate Cory: 1905–1912*, Albuquerque: University of New Mexico Press, 1988.

Suzanne Benally, Navajo/Santa Clara, was born in New Mexico. As an educator, she is politically and philosophically committed to multicultural education, alternative experiential education, and the goal of making the educational needs and voices of Native Americans heard. As a writer of poetry and essays, she draws upon her cultural and spiritual knowledge and experiences. Her home is on the Navajo Nation but she currently works and lives in Boulder, Colorado.

Jimmie Durham, Wolf Clan Cherokee, is a poet, essayist, sculptor, and performance-and-installation artist, born in Nevada County, Arkansas, in 1940. After a stint in the navy, and after art school (in Geneva), Durham joined the American Indian Movement in 1972 and was founding director of the International Indian Treaty Council. He has been editor of the journal *Art & Artists* and writes occasionally for *Artforum.* He exhibits internationally and has had one-man shows in New York, London, and Derry (Ireland); most recently, he was represented in the 1992 Dokumenta, in Kassel. His poetry is collected in a book, *Columbus Day* (1983).

Rayna Green, Cherokee, is director of the American Indian Program at the National Museum of American History. Known for her work in museum exhibition, video, and performance production, she also writes extensively on American Indian women and American culture. Her most recent book is *American Indian Women in American Indian Society*, (1991), a work for young adults as well as a general audience.

Joy Harjo was born in Tulsa, Oklahoma, in 1951 and is an enrolled member of the Creek Tribe. She is a graduate of the Institute of American Indian Arts and the University of New Mexico, and received an M.F.A. in creative writing from the Iowa Writer's Workshop (1978). She has published four books of poetry, including *She Had Some Horses* and *In Mad Love and War.* In 1990 she collaborated with photographer and astronomer Stephen Strom on *Secrets from the Center of the World.* She is on the steering committee of the En'owkin Centre International School of Writing (for Native Americans) and travels extensively, giving readings and lectures.

She has won numerous awards, including the Josephine Miles Award for Excellence in Literature from PEN (Oakland), the William Carlos Williams Award from the Poetry Society of America, and the Delmore Schwartz Award from New York University. Harjo is also a screenwriter, plays saxophone with her band Poetic Justice, and has produced many features, including *Apache Mountain Spirits*, for Silvercloud Video Productions. She is currently professor of creative writing at the University of New Mexico.

Lucy R. Lippard is a writer and activist who lives in New York City, Boulder, Colorado, and Georgetown, Maine. She is the author of a novel, *I See/You Mean*, and fifteen books on contemporary art, the most recent of which is *Mixed Blessings: New Art in a Multicultural America* (1990).

Gerald McMaster, Plains Cree, was born and grew up near North Battleford, on the Red Pheasant Reserve, in Saskatchewan. He studied at the Institute of American Indian Art in Santa Fe, New Mexico, and the Minneapolis College of Art and Design. He is currently curator of contemporary Indian art at the Canadian Museum of Civilization, Hull, Quebec, and an internationally exhibited painter.

Jolene Rickard was born less than a mile from the brink of the waterfalls at Niagara in 1956. Two years later, the U.S. government took nearly half the territories of her people, the Tuscarora, for the Robert Moses Power Project, to provide more electrical current for the thousand points of light burning today. She was raised by her father, who is Bear Clan, and her mother, who is Turtle Clan, to respect all living things, but not the United States or its flag. Rickard is currently pursuing a Ph.D. in American studies at the University of Buffalo, New York, and she writes on the issues of identity construction and representation. Her photography has been exhibited widely in the last decade and she was chosen for the last Heard Museum Biennial in Phoenix. She recently completed a residency at Lightworks in Rochester and is on the board of the Center for Exploratory and Perceptual Art (CEPA), in Buffalo. Rickard is married, lives on the Tuscarora Nation, and does all this for her daughter, Mia, and her niece, Zan.

Ramona Sakiestewa is a contemporary tapestry weaver born and raised in the American Southwest. Most of her family live at Hopi or in the Phoenix and Albuquerque areas. She has written many articles about weaving, has had one-woman shows at the Wheelright Museum (Santa Fe) and the Newark Museum, and has won awards at Indian Market (Santa Fe). She has reproduced two ancient Anasazi feather tapestries for the Bandelier National Monument and has also woven the work of other contemporary artists, including Frank Lloyd Wright and Kenneth Noland. She has been executive director of Atlatl, and Minority Affairs Coordinator for the New Mexico Arts Division. Sakiestewa has lived and worked in New York, Mexico City, Peru, Japan, China, and has traveled throughout Europe. She lives in Santa Fe with her husband, the poet Arthur Sze, and their son, Micah.

David Seals (Davydd ap Saille) is a descendent of the Huron prophet Deganawidah, who wrote the famous charter of the Iroquois Confederacy. He is the author of novels—*The Powwow Highway*, *Third Eye Theatre*, and *Sweet Medicine*—and a collection of essays and poems, *The Poetic College*. He lives in the Black Hills.

Leslie Marmon Silko was born in Albuquerque in 1948 of mixed ancestry—Laguna Pueblo, Mexican, and white. She grew up in Laguna Pueblo and now lives in Tucson. Silko is the author of the poetry and prose work *Storyteller* and the novels *Ceremony* and *Almanac of the Dead*. Her stories have appeared in numerous magazines and collections and she is the recipient of a MacArthur Foundation Grant.

Jaune Quick-To-See Smith is an internationally exhibited painter whose work appears in numerous publications and is the subject of several films. An activist-spokesperson for contemporary Native American artists, she is an enrolled member of the Flathead Tribe, in Montana, and has founded two cooperatives: Coup Marks, on the Flathead Reserve, and Grey Canyon Artists, in Albuquerque. She lectures widely and has recently received several public art commissions around the country. Smith has curated numerous exhibitions of Native American art, including the currently traveling "Our Land, Ourselves" and "The Submuloc Show, or The Columbus Wohs." She serves or has served on the boards of the Institute for American Indian Art (Santa Fe), American Indian Contemporary Art Gallery (San Francisco), Montana Indian Contemporary Arts, Atlatl (Phoenix), and the College Art Association.

Paul Chaat Smith is Comanche. He left Antioch College for South Dakota in August 1974 to handle press operations for the Wounded Knee Legal Defense/Offense Committee. In 1979 he became founding editor of *The Treaty Council News*, the newsletter of the American Indian Movement International Indian Treaty Council. In 1979 he moved to New York City, where he took a position with the Funding Exchange and began to write for various publications. In 1990 Smith left the